FACEBOOK ADVERTISING 2019

The Ultimate Guide on Facebook ads and Tips to Succed on Instagram, Youtube and Twitter, Advertise your Brand, Grow your Social Media

Jack Gary

reserved.

Furthermore, the information that can be found within the pages described forthwith shall be considered both accurate and truthful when it comes to the recounting of facts. As such, any use, correct or incorrect, of the provided information will render the Publisher free of responsibility as to the actions taken outside of their direct purview. Regardless, there are zero scenarios where the original author or the Publisher can be deemed liable in any fashion for any damages or hardships that may result from any of the information discussed herein.

Additionally, the information in the following pages is intended only for informational purposes and should thus be thought of as universal. As befitting its nature, it is presented without assurance regarding its prolonged validity or interim quality. Trademarks that are mentioned are done without written consent and can in no way be considered an endorsement from the trademark holder.

TABLE OF CONTENTS

INTRODUCTION

It is not a secret that in this day and age, if you own a business, you should leverage the power of the internet to increase your revenue. The best channel to do this? Facebook. This is why we decided to create this book to help business owners and entrepreneurs to take their social media marketing game to the next level.

But first, let's take a look at what social media marketing really is because there is a lot of confusion around this topic.

People today interact with brands through social media. Therefore, having a strong social presence and being able to adequately tell the story of your brand is the key to creating empathy and loyalty. If implemented correctly, social media marketing can help your company achieve your growth and reputation goals.

What is Social Media Marketing?

Social media marketing, or SMM, is a form of web marketing that uses a series of social media platforms in order to obtain a profitable and empathetic online advertising communication with users. Social media marketing retains users and customers by sharing textual content, images, and viral videos.

This book was created to provide useful information on social media marketing aimed at improving its business, giving and accommodating businesses an operational tool with great advertising potentials at reduced costs. By reading this book, you can start developing your social media marketing plan in a more professional way.

Social Media Marketing: Start with a Plan

Before starting to create a social media marketing campaign on Facebook, Instagram, YouTube, and other social media sites, you need to consider your sales and branding goals. Starting a social media marketing campaign without a strategic plan is like walking through a forest without a map: you will get lost.

Create a social media marketing plan and reflect on the goals to be achieved:

- What do you hope to achieve through social media marketing?

- What is your target audience?

- Where can you contact this target audience and how do you use social media?

- What message do you want to send to your target audience?

Social Media Marketing: Develop Goals

Social media marketing can help you achieve a number of goals, such as:

- Increased traffic profiled towards your company website

- Increase in leads and conversions

- Increase of brand awareness

- Creating a brand identity and a positive image of the brand (brand reputation)

- Communicate and interact empathically with your customers

The Best Tips to Learn Marketing with Social Media

Here are some social media marketing tips to get your bearings right during all social media campaigns:

Planning – As mentioned earlier, building a social media marketing plan is essential. It is necessary to identify the keywords, ideas, and contents that could be of interest to the target audience.

Content is the most important factor – As with other areas of online marketing, content is the most important thing when it comes to social media marketing. Be sure to provide interesting and viral information to your customers. Create different types of content using images, videos, and infographics, as well as classic content marketing.

Be consistent – Using social media for marketing allows your company to advertise brands and products across a wide range of channels. Although each platform has its own unique environment, the core of your online communication must remain similar for all channels.

Blog – A blog is a great tool for social media marketing that allows you to share a wide range of information and valuable content for readers. Your company blog can also serve as a social media marketing blog, thus creating a place to highlight your company's activities.

Link – Although the use of social media for marketing is mainly based on the unique and original sharing of content concerning its business, it is also excellent for linking external articles to gain more followers and fans. If other sources provide information that you think is valuable to your target audience, it is useful to create a dedicated link. The connection to external sources improves trust and reliability, and it is also possible to receive the same favor.

Keeping track of competitors – It's always important to keep an eye on your competitors who can provide valuable data on keyword searches, links to the business, and other important information. If your competitors are using a certain social media marketing technique that seems to work for them, you just have to do the same thing, but better.

Since Facebook stores data about its users which are entered spontaneously in their profile (e.g. age, location, interests), it has a very good idea of who its users are and what they are interested in. For example, just put a like on a football page to make them understand that you are following this sport.

You will understand then that the potential of subjecting these well-defined users to targeted advertisements is enormous.

In the past years, social media has become one of the most effective advertising channels, being able to get new leads (contacts) and turn them into paying customers.

Facebook Ads works in both B2C and B2B and there are

many cases that show an increase in results, even 5 times, after taking advantage of advertising on Facebook.

The growth of Facebook is steady. Both in terms of new users and marketing opportunities, and the budgets dedicated to the AD on social media have doubled worldwide in the last 2 years, from $16 billion in 2014 to $31 billion in 2016. In 2018, analysts expect a further increase of 26.3%.

To all of these, add that the number of active users every day on Facebook was about 1.23 billion people in 2017 and on average each of these spends 50 minutes a day between Facebook, Instagram, and Messenger. With Facebook Ads, you can reach each of these users with highly customizable targets such as interests, demographics, locations, actions performed on a website, and much more.

Do you own a small business and want to start a Social Media Marketing activity this 2019 to promote your business? If the answer is yes (and it should be), here are the 10 rules to follow to get success:

1. Do not improvise. Before opening your social media accounts and starting to publish, analyze the target audience and, on the basis of its characteristics, realize a strategy that provides the guidelines to follow in all areas of communication from the choice of channels to the definition of contents.

2. Give the public what they want. Create quality content, provide information, advice, and create curiosity that can really interest and engage your audience.

3. Do not be too promotional. Avoid talking only about your company or your products. The goal of social networks is to create conversations. Do not make classic advertising.

4. Interacting. Respond quickly to questions or comments from your audience. Through social media, you must create human and real relationships.

5. Publish constantly. Stick to an editorial calendar that provides for a periodic and constant publication based on your availability.

6. Monitor the market. Try to stay up-to-date on changes in your target market to change your strategy based on new trends or needs.

   1. **Define evaluation metrics.** What do you want to achieve with your social activity? Increase your visibility? Increase sales? Get leads? Based on your goals, define the most appropriate metrics for evaluating the results.

   2. **Monitor the results.** Analyze the behavior of your audience, interactions with your social accounts, and visits to the site. Once the metrics have been defined, constantly check that the results obtained are in line with those expected and, if not, make some strategic changes.

   3. **Do not be in a hurry.** Social Media Marketing does not provide immediate results, but it is an activity that requires competence, patience, and, above all, constancy.

   4. **"1 is greater than 0 or is it?"** Accounts not updated

are a risk to the company's online reputation. So, if you have little time available, avoid opening a thousand different social pages and then abandoning them. Alternatively, you can contact external consultants who, on the basis of your specific needs, will be able to optimize your Social Media Marketing activity.

These are just a few basic principles that will guide you through the course of this book.

Now, it is time to dive deeper into the topic and discover all the secrets of Facebook advertising and social media marketing. We are sure that if you follow the advice and strategies presented in this book, you will have a bright future in front of you.

Chapter 1:

WHAT IS SOCIAL MEDIA MARKETING?

FACEBOOK, INSTAGRAM, YOUTUBE, AND TWITTER

For how often this is presented, the answer to the question "Is social media marketing this year?" is still "It depends". You have to ask yourself what your goals are and, once the mechanisms of advertising on Facebook are understood, the answer will be obvious to you.

If you want to intercept an audience that might be interested in your product or service, surely Facebook Ads will be for you. It will allow you to submit your ads to a specific target of users.

If you have traffic on your site or e-commerce, regardless of how it is obtained, you may want to recontact those users to repropose your ads.

Do you know that when you are looking for a product and after visiting a site, you will find yourself the sponsored ads later when going to Facebook?

It's called retargeting. You will be able to create customized user lists based on their actions, such as visiting a particular page (article, product, landing page, shopping cart, etc.) and exploiting them for well-targeted ads.

It will be essential to have a very clear strategy for our Facebook Ads campaign. It will be appropriate to understand where the potential customer is located within our sales funnel and submit different ads depending on whether it is far or near the purchase.

We certainly cannot offer the same ad to a potential customer who does not know our brand and someone that already has our product in his chart. This is just to say that Facebook has great potential for small businesses but needs to be used properly to get the most out of it.

Do you really need a Social Media Marketing Plan? The answer is simple, short, and direct: if you do not have a plan, you have a little chance of success. Planning means making a strategy; without a strategy in the modern market, you do not sell. Planning means selling.

But is creating a true Social Media Marketing Plan easy or difficult? It depends if, for you, it is the first time you can find some difficulties, but you will see in concrete that it is not very far from what you have already done in the past for your business. You have to reflect, compare, hypothesize, choose, understand, enhance, and, finally, to verify.

Using a metaphor, we could see Marketing as an orchestra and the Social Media Marketing Plan as the score to be followed. Every marketing action is the symphony played by a single musician where the score imposes rules, times, and style. The orchestra represents the set of many instruments that play, but they play alternately. With a wise strategy, every musical instrument is important but necessary only if it follows the score. It is the conductor who decides what, when, and why.

Now, are you ready to make a Social Media Marketing Plan? Did you understand the need? To achieve a good plan you have to follow these 6 steps for they will simplify your life:

Step 1: Identify the Correct Goals

The first step for any marketing strategy is to establish the goals you are hoping to achieve. The more you have clear objectives to achieve, the easier it will be to achieve them or to react quickly to changes in the market and business strategies. Without a concrete objective, there is no means to measure the progress of a marketing campaign. These Social goals must, of course, be aligned with the broader marketing strategy.

One of the most used methods to identify the correct objective to pursue is the SMART approach. SMART is an acronym used to remember the 5 characteristics of the correct objective: specific (Specific), measurable (Measurable), attainable (Attainable), pertinent (Relevant), limited in time (Time-bound, with a fixed expiration).

An easy way to start your social media marketing plan is to give yourself at least two to three small goals. For example, you decide that you will share photos about the corporate culture on Instagram. You'll do this by sending 3 photos a week, with the goal of getting at least 30 shares a week and 10 comments. In addition, post your short articles on Facebook (at least twice a week), better if related to content on your site or blog, because you can directly link them and receive more visits. All activities must have a pre-established time and must be measurable and measured.

Step 2: Market Analysis and Competition Analysis

The second step is to do a real market analysis of what can be done on every single social network and what your competitors are doing, obviously taking inspiration from international success stories, perhaps from your own sector.

Step 3: Voice and Style

Each company has its own style and its own image that is usually reflected in every action: how the sales show up, the stand presented at the fair, the brochures, the business cards, the website, and so on. The company canNOT communicate; it simply does so with its headquarters and warehouse, through furniture, colors, and its logo. The actions on social networks must invariably communicate the style and the image that the company has strategically chosen to communicate. The Marketing Manager must be able to make social users perceive what the company wants them to perceive.

Step 4: The Tools and the Channels

When you are well aware of the company style to communicate, all you need to do is to identify the tools and channels you want to use. For example: LinkedIn and Facebook to create ad hoc posts on company products and services, Twitter to convey content with links to blog posts and website, Instagram to communicate photographs about corporate style, and Pinterest both to communicate style and infographics on company services and the technologies identified.

Among the tools, we must obviously include the Web Tools that were born in recent years, dedicated to the editorial management of content on social media. Well-known tools such as HootSuite, TweetDeck,

ManageFlitter, and many others are essential for the management and analysis of social media marketing.

Step 5: Editorial Calendar (Content Plan)

The fifth step gives you the opportunity to reassemble all the previous steps in a single tool, creating a real Content Plan, with precise timing divided by days, weeks, and months.

The editorial calendar must reflect the identified objectives, the chosen market strategy, the company style, and the pre-established tools/channels (in the photo above: an example of a simple calendar, developed in Excel).

For example, if your purpose on Instagram is to generate contacts, and the one on Facebook simply to communicate the corporate image, you must make sure that your calendar represents well these two objectives (in terms of timing, type of message, tool used, editorial consistency over time, and number of weekly posts).

Step 6: Constant Check

Having implemented a Social Media Marketing Plan with its editorial strategy, it becomes crucial to be able to measure its progress and success, perhaps even ROI (return on investment). Also for this step, as for the fourth, it is essential to use dedicated tools—first of all is Google Analytics (analysis blog, website, newsletter, landing pages, etc.). For some time, Twitter has also been offering its Analytics for free. These and other tools allow you to analyze in detail a large amount of data grouped by type, bringing a clear picture of what works and what does not, which social media leads to more visits to the website and which others can turn them into active contacts (customers).

ADVANTAGES AND DISADVANTAGES OF SOCIAL MEDIA MARKETING

How much do ads cost? How is the price established?

It is the most frequent question in this environment, but unfortunately, there is no answer other than "it depends".

On what does it depend? From what you are advertising to who your target is, how many competitors there are, and what your goals are, just to mention some aspects.

Before reaching the total costs of a Facebook campaign, it is important to understand how these costs are established. Unlike traditional advertising methods, Facebook does not have a fixed price for each placement but follows a system of an auction among advertisers to get the ad published. This is because Facebook users can only see a limited number of ads per day.

There are various factors that determine which ad will be displayed, who will be shown and at what cost:

- *Who you are targeting*: As we will see later, the possibilities of targeting are many and depending on the target you choose, you will compete with other advertisers.

- *Your relevance score, engagement, and click-through rate*: Facebook assigns to each ad a score of relevance from 1 to 10 depending on the associated target and its response. The higher the interaction and the number of clicks are, the higher your score will be and the more likely your ad will be displayed at lower costs.

- *The timing*: The more competitive the sector is, the higher the costs will be. There will be periods of the year, such as during certain holidays, where costs could increase significantly. You can choose from various options, but which one is best will depend on your campaign objectives.

You can pay in various ways:

- *Per impression*: Pay for each display of your ad. It is better to use this option when you want to reach as many people as possible. For example, in a brand awareness campaign.

- *Per click*: Pay only if someone clicks on your ad. This option is preferable when we want to take users to click on a link that will take them to the site or to a specific landing page.

- *Per action*: Pay only when a user performs a certain action, how to fill out an entry form, buy a product, or visit a certain page. With this option, the most social network will show ads to people who are more likely to take one of these actions.

So, you will understand that answering the question "How much does it cost?" is complex. The important thing is to set a budget and manage it in the best way possible, reaching potential customers in a careful manner, and keeping an eye on the really relevant parameters, such as cost per conversion. Not knowing what you will spend is one of the main disadvantages of Facebook marketing, but still, it is something that can be overcome easily.

A lot of people that approach social media marketing for the first time think that the key is to be on every social network. The truth, however, is that it is much better to focus only on the platforms that people use the most. Right now, Instagram, Facebook, and YouTube are the most used social networks, so we will focus on those three.

INSTAGRAM

Available at first only for iOS devices, the version for Android was born in 2012, allowing a faster deployment of the application and a significant increase in the number of subscribers to the platform. It is only as a result of this great growth that Zuckerberg understands its potential, so much that he decided to buy it to turn Instagram into a powerful social network, almost as long as the longest running Facebook.

According to the Instagram blog, in June 2018, registered users were 1 billion, and the data continues to grow. This makes us understand that Instagram is a social network not yet saturated and with much more to give to its users, so it proves a suitable platform for the development of new strategies of social media marketing—thanks to the use of visual storytelling with the aid of the many new features offered by the developers.

How to Succeed on Instagram

Instagram is a rather unusual social networking platform, unlike how other social networks such as Facebook or Twitter prevails. Thanks also to the lower average age of users, a more informal behavior characterized by immediacy and sharing of the moment.

Instagram is, therefore, increasingly used in synergy with other social networks to highlight the "behind the scenes" of the brand—a less serious part of the brand linked to the story, to people, and to life. This is also to show a more "creative" side, linked to the playful and artistic aspect.

Using a Business Account

Business profiles arrived in America in June 2016 and brought very useful news for all companies that use Instagram in their social media marketing strategy.

If you are a freelancer or a company, if you have not

already done so, we recommend to immediately turn on the switch. Simply enter the settings and tap on "Switch to Business Profile". At this point, you will not have to do anything but associate the linked Facebook page and indicate the contact options such as email and phone number.

By providing this data correctly, users will be able to contact you directly without too many steps when they will land on your Business profile: just tap on "Call" or "Email". In addition, for the companies that have activated the Instagram shopping function, the item "Products" will appear.

Once the switch is made to Business Profile, at the top right, a graphic icon will appear, namely the Insights.

The data shown are as follows:

- Impression and reach of your posts;

- Photos with more interactions;

- Insights data on Instagram Stories;

- Data on followers; and

- Insights related to promotions.

INSTAGRAM BIOGRAPHY: HOW TO WRITE IT

To implement a marketing strategy on Instagram, it is necessary to start from the details that are the care of the bio field.

It is important to know that within this section, it is

mandatory to be as clear as possible, using the keywords that best identify the sector to which the company belongs. Recently, the platform introduced the possibility of inserting hashtags into the bio which make profiles easier to find.

The Instagram biography can contain a maximum of 150 characters and must be written with extreme care because, together with the profile image, this is what will prompt the user to click on the "Follow" button and on the call to action.

Tone of Voice (ToV)

First of all, it is necessary to define a tone of voice consistent with the values of the brand but which is in line with the target audience—the potential members of the community. To define the tone of voice, it is necessary to build a social media monitoring activity, which is the monitoring of user conversations.

This type of activity can be verified through suitable online tools such as Radian6, Socialbakers Suite, and many others.

Listening to conversations that revolve around certain keywords useful for your Instagram Marketing strategy will be of fundamental importance to understand how users express themselves and what problems and needs they would like to see resolved. All of these are essential when studying a digital communication strategy.

Emojis

The use of emoji is by no means a child's practice, but, on the contrary, they can be used as a creative list for the division of application fields.

The visual content attracts much more than the text, consequently putting emoticons that help to outline the bio, which is a way to get the user's attention.

Another trick is to wrap between sentences, so as to better clarify who you are, what you do, and then call to action to the user.

Call to Action (CTA)

In an Instagram Marketing strategy, it is always necessary to include a clear call to action to users. "Visit our website" or "Follow us on Facebook and Twitter" are CTAs in all respects, and it is necessary that the message is clear to users and traceable to the company using for example a tracking code of Google Analytics.

THE IMPORTANCE OF STORYTELLING

Why has visual storytelling become fundamental in any digital strategy? It is clear: recent research has shown that users have an average attention threshold of 8 seconds. This shows the need for companies to be able to create attractive tools to ensure that the user's eye stops to read and watch content.

Storytelling means telling stories for persuasive communication, especially in politics, economics, and business. With the advent of social networks, users want to read and see original stories. This is why companies are required continuous innovation in the art of storytelling and emotion.

Self-referencing does not pay any more: it is necessary to

use tools like Instagram to create narrative universes useful for community involvement.

To be able to create a good strategy for Instagram Marketing, it is of fundamental importance to experiment to find the correct and most appreciated way by the users. The feed created must be homogeneous so as not to confuse the community, which means that if you deal with catering, it makes no sense to publish travel content or other topics not closely related.

To have a good following on Instagram, you have to start from a good visual content: if the content is interesting and engaging, users will stop to read the caption, or notice the caption. Within this field, it is necessary to tell stories involving the microblogging technique.

Instagram, like Facebook, offers fairly frequent news, such as 60-second videos, Instagram Stories, photo albums, and IGTV: this is why it is always experimenting with new techniques for creating engagement within the community.

Speaking of 60-second videos, if you have included them in your strategy, we recommend using Instagram video apps like Boomerang, Diptic, or Flipagram.

CREATE A CONTENT MARKETING STRATEGY ON INSTAGRAM

The first thing to do once we have identified our target audience is to structure the right content marketing strategy.

In fact, it is not enough to "be on Instagram" to be able

to say you use this medium. Rather, it is necessary to study a creative path that allows the user who follows the brand to receive interesting contents, obviously respecting the tone of voice and the image and positioning of the company, and that, through this path, we can bring user to become an ambassador and customer of the company.

To give a concrete (and simple) example: if the company is in the food sector, you will have to create a content marketing strategy that aims to give culinary directions such as recipes, ingredients, and raw materials. The contents should not be strictly related to the sale of the product but must serve to create an interaction and a relationship of trust with the user, who will then be interested in accessing the social network also because it finds interesting content on the company feed.

CREATE AN EDITORIAL PLAN AND AN EDITORIAL CALENDAR

Once a clear content marketing strategy has been identified, shared with all team members, we can proceed to summarize what has been decided so far within the editorial plan for the social network. It means creating a document with objectives, targets, and ways of creating content within a document that becomes the guide to consistently create future content to be posted on Instagram.

These contents will be programmed and inserted into an editorial calendar. Having an editorial calendar is essential because it allows you to never run out of content, as these are decided on time, with certain deadlines and with equally certain managers.

An editorial calendar is, therefore, made up of specific posts, inserted into a weekly and monthly calendar, to be followed to make sure you never run out of posts. Ideally, if we believe we have enough content, we could also post on Instagram every day, which means structuring an editorial calendar that needs to have several months already covered. It is, however, desirable to have a calendar that requires posting two or three times a week.

INTERACT WITH FOLLOWERS AND CREATE A COMMUNITY

Creating a community on Instagram is very important to create a Comment Marketing activity, a strategy based on comments on photos similar to those published by your company. The use of Instagram Bot is increasingly frequent, allowing follow-up and commenting based on who uses specific hashtags within the caption.

The problem of Comment Marketing with the Bots is that it does not lead to the real creation of the community, as a simple "Nice" or a little heart is not enough to really interact with the relevant public. For this reason, for the creation of a community, it is always better to search through a photo hashtag in line with your brand and to comment on them manually and regularly, writing something that also leads to an answer and intrigues the user so much to push them to follow you in turn.

HOW TO USE INFLUENCERS

What are the influencers? Influencers are people with a

significant following on Instagram, who may then have the power to direct users who follow them to a particular brand or company.

In fact, influencers are usually rather sectorial and followed assiduously by those who are interested in a specific topic, so they can contact to look for a relationship with their own brand if the target between their followers and those of the company is coherent. You can structure a co-marketing strategy with a shared hashtag or, in the case of companies in the fashion industry, for example, use them as brand ambassadors through their posts. In case of events (such as festivals or other events), they can be invited to create awareness on the specific event.

CREATE CONTEST ON INSTAGRAM

The creation of a contest on Instagram is a very widespread practice to stimulate the engagement in the community already formed for the improvement of the brand awareness and for the generation of new qualified leads.

STIMULATING COMPETITION

For participation in an Instagram contest, users must feel encouraged to share personal photographs with a decidedly large network. In order to convince and involve the community, it is necessary to have a stimulating idea that will somehow leverage the emotional sphere of the individual.

An example of an emotional contest can be that of

Vetoquinol, where users have been asked to take up moments of play and fun with their four-legged friend.

INTERESTING PRIZES

When users decide to participate in an online competition, it is very easy for them to try to win the prize at stake. The greater the perceived value (economic and/or affective), the greater the chances of participation by users.

If the company deals with sales of technological products, the raffling of the latest tablet model released on the market will be more incentive than the awarding of simple custom covers.

Furthermore, the prizes of competition must always be in line with the promoter's core business to avoid confusing users about your field of activity.

STUDYING A PROMOTION STRATEGY

In addition to the classic promotional strategies, such as ADV, newsletters, postings on the page, and shares on Instagram, you can use the hashtags. Each competition must have its own hashtag designed for the occasion, which allows to group in a simple way all the contents published by the users.

INSTAGRAM STORIES: HOW TO EXPLOIT THEM

The Instagram Stories were introduced in the second half of 2016, after witnessing the Snapchat boom especially in the very young audience (target between 15 and 25 years).

The Stories have potentials, thanks to their usability: they serve to offer special contents that disappear after 24 hours. Applied to Instagram Marketing can be very useful, as you can create exclusive content for creating engagement within particular communities.

For example, you can use them to show moments of exclusive events to engage the fan base or to offer special discounts and promotions lasting only 24 hours. Or again, if you have a verified Instagram profile, you will have the opportunity to show the products offered by the online shop by entering the direct link, this way you will not require too many steps to users, who will feel more incentive to proceed with the purchase.

This technique is often used by blogger and entrepreneur Chiara Ferragni, who, in her stories, mixes moments of everyday life with decidedly more commercial content in which she shows the products she designed and created, referring directly to her e-shop.

Features like questions, surveys, and emoji appreciation have made them even more interactive, contributing to the enormous success that Instagram Stories are having between users and companies.

How to Measure the Results

Created that the strategy for the Instagram profile is useful, set goals and periodically check if those objectives—medium-term and long-term—have been respected. You will then check, in addition to the mere and simple "engagement" on the platform, if those followers have also become customers or users of our product.

In order to measure the results, it is important to have

correctly set the conversion funnel and be able to obtain quantifiable data from the analytics platforms set. If the goal is to make sure that users register for a service on our site, it will be important to identify how many users have come through our Instagram channel.

FACEBOOK

In 2018, Facebook remains one of the main channels for marketing. But, like everything in the digital world, it changes regularly and every so often. At the beginning of this year, Facebook changed the algorithm of its News Feed, deciding to prioritize the posts of relatives and friends (the system considers the profiles with which a user contacts more often), to those that cause discussions and conversations and to the publication of the pages that a user has chosen to see first (See First in the preferences of the News Feed). Under these conditions, marketing on Facebook becomes a challenge.

YOUTUBE

YouTube is a web-based video sharing platform that was set up 11 years ago by the trio Hurley, Karim, and Chen. The idea of creating a social video sharing platform was particularly risky but diabolically apt.

What at the time was simply an idea, a website, in a few years has become the reference point for millions of Internet users who upload movies of any kind every day, while millions of users spend their time watching these videos every day.

The growth of YouTube has become exponential when

the giant of Mountain View, Google, has decided to acquire the company and liquidate the three founders handsomely.

The commercial operation turned out to be a winner. Google, in fact, has made YouTube the third most visited website in the world, behind only the same search engine of Google to the social network par excellence Facebook.

Since YouTube has come to life and has become what it is today, we have studied the phenomenon and our goal is to promote and give visibility to our customers also through this colossus of social media.

To date, YouTube is a hotbed of new talent, music, and entertainment in general and is an immense advertising window for companies and individuals who have chosen the Internet as a vehicle to promote their product and their professionalism.

The promotion through YouTube will be one of the biggest opportunities that this social platform makes available this year and through the right skills, we will know how to enhance and take the best of what YouTube offers us.

Success comes through YouTube views, visits obtained by watching that specific video or that specific channel.

In this case, every user registered on the platform, (after the marriage with Google, just a Big G account), can become in one fell swoop, publisher, author, director, and screenwriter of their YouTube channel, which will be instantly reachable throughout the world and official disseminator of your ideas. Or you can decide to become simply a spectator with decidedly active connotations, since you can decide, together with many other viewers, which means the success of a video or of the same YouTube channel and also a reflection of a brand or an idea.

The YouTube views are, therefore, the amount of views that the video gets, not to be confused with the YouTube Likes, which instead indicate your liking related to the video or channel viewed.

The second concept is not entirely different from what made Facebook famous and is one of the first parameters to keep in mind to achieve success.

Making a video and uploading it to YouTube is easy, but it is even easier to end up in obscurity and never reach the desired visibility.

Our goal is to provide the right information not to end up in a dead end and not remain anonymous.

Whether you are a company or a private individual with a new idea, we have the means of promotion for your YouTube Marketing and we can offer you a solid marketing plan.

As with any product, even YouTube has its own good rules and its good techniques to stay on the crest of the wave, and we study and apply it daily.

YouTube SEO has some basic steps to follow, not to be one of many on the video sharing platform, but to be among the protagonists, offering greater visibility on search engines.

Among the measures made available, we mention some that may seem trivial, but they are all important to get to the top and stay there.

The metadata is undoubtedly fundamental, that is all the additional information we can give as a part of our video. The descriptions to the video and to the YouTube Channel are an example, but subtitles can also be used, if present, as an indexing parameter for a video (the same speech is intended to be extended in the same way between channel and video).

Accurate description in the process of creating the channel (uploading the video, in short) should not be taken lightly, but rather must be carefully studied and weighted.

It is the place where billions of people place their eyes every day. The interesting fact is that these eyes do not belong only to a particular category of people, but to every population.

You will certainly understand what this could mean for your company's marketing. But how do you effectively use this channel to promote and grow your business? Let's browse a bit between the channels of this social network and see what we can understand.

YouTube is full of quirky videos, often frivolous and sometimes meaningless (at least in appearance), uploaded mainly by teenagers or young adults.

TIP 1: Publish Content, Not Advertisement

You'll soon realize that traditional forms of advertising do not work on YouTube. You'll have to experiment with other ways to advertise your e-commerce, your site, or your company.

Not even company presentation videos or product demos do not give great results unless they are particularly creative.

When you create video content to upload to this channel, take time to reflect on why and how your audience should appreciate it and share it. The shareability factor is indeed as important as the underlying idea and the quality of its realization.

TIP 2: Become the Face of Your Business

YouTube is a community of real people who want to give in, feel, and interact with other real people. The link with your company or with your brand is greatly strengthened if the public can associate a face, preferably the most representative of the entire organization.

This move can profoundly change the dynamics of interaction, going from watching a company video to building a relationship with a human being. Aiming at the establishment of interpersonal relationships, therefore, becomes a long-term strategy that can make your company gain life for customers.

The face of the company must obviously appear as much as possible in the videos, in the header of your channel, and in the previews of the contents. Another winning strategic move is to include splits of personal life within your business if there is not too much forcing. Allow your audience to peek behind the scenes, to see your project take shape, or to discover how you started this profession.

This transparency adds depth and color to your marketing.

HINT 3: All Come from Zero

Many users, who begin to use YouTube for their company's marketing open a channel, upload a couple of content and soon get discouraged because they do not achieve the desired goals in terms of subscriptions and views. From the initial enthusiasm, they pass to abandon the enterprise with a fair load of frustration.

Gathering an audience around your YouTube channel is a process that takes time and patience. Focus on creating valuable content and in the best possible quality. Promote your channel: announce it on your blog, on your mailing lists, and on the other social platforms where you are present. Also, include a YouTube sharing button in the above-the-fold area of your website.

As you do everything in your power to promote your channel and videos, remember to interact with the followers you've already won. Take care of these people who, in a boundless sea of possibilities, have chosen to follow you: reply to any postman comments—even if possible on the Community—as soon as possible. If they have a channel, visit it and comment on it in turn.

HINT 4: Bring Users to Your Site

For most businesses, a YouTube Marketing strategy cannot stop attracting subscribers and views. Of course, this is the first of the goals, but once achieved, there must be a further step towards converting these users into customers. To do this, you will probably need to create a bridge between YouTube and your site.

Include a link to your site in the first line of each description you write for your videos.

Enter a link to the About Us section of your site in the header of your channel.

Study methods for making the user move to your site, such as a two-part video of which the first is available on YouTube and the second only on one of your company web pages.

TIP 5: Find Collaborations

Another very effective tactic to empower your efforts on YouTube is to collaborate with an established designer. This can happen in different ways and forms, but for most companies, it will probably involve investing a certain budget to offer to one of the well-targeted YouTube videos for your goals.

Take some time to select candidates. Choose between those who have at least 100,000 subscribers and who exercise a significant ascendancy on your target audience. Once you have identified your influencer, you can make different proposals: create a video according to your requests, appear in one of your videos, and/or talk about yourself or your products in one of his productions.

These characters are generally very protective of their community and the role they have won. They are understandably very selective in evaluating the opportunities for collaboration that they receive. Offer them something that they can genuinely feel in their chords and you will be more likely to receive positive feedback.

HINT 6: SEO is Important

YouTube is the second largest search engine after Google–which is also a brother since 2006—and the two get along very well. Although the Google algorithm is almost top secret, it seems that a YouTube video with the appropriate metadata compiled properly has more ease to acquire a high ranking compared to a blog post equally optimized.

Not only can your videos appear among Google search results, they also do so with a thumbnail that provides a visual preview of the content.

TIP 7: Do Not Forget the Call to Action

This is an essential point when it comes to using YouTube for professional reasons. If it is possible during, but no doubt, at the end of each video, you need to insert a call to action: you want your users to take a certain action, once your creation is appreciated, right?

The content is, in fact, a tool to capture the attention, perhaps entertain, inform, and create a relationship. At a certain point, however, this attention should flow into something that will also benefit your business. This could be simply filling out a form, sharing the video with your contacts, or visiting a specific page of your e-commerce.

The possibilities are endless and the effectiveness of your choice will also depend on the creativity that you will be able to use in catching them. Consult YouTube policies, make sure your idea is not in opposition to any of the points and then give free space to your inventiveness.

GROWING YOUR YOUTUBE BUSINESS

YouTube registers more than a billion unique visitors each month. In the same amount of time, over 6 billion hours of content are used by users: it is clear that, for brands as well as creators, YouTube is an opportunity not to be missed to present, tell, and connect with the public.

Building your presence on the Mountain View video platform cannot disregard the design of a channel that, by structure and content, can attract users and encourage them to subscribe.

Notwithstanding that the quality of the contents remains an unavoidable prerogative to achieve this goal, below you will find a list of 13 useful things to do to promote your channel and increase subscribers on YouTube.

1. Promotion on Other Social Channels

Every social network has its own nature, characteristics, languages, and communicative modalities of its own, often different public. Choosing to publish the same content on multiple platforms does not always pay in terms of effectiveness: however, using your own "social spaces" to promote the YouTube channel can be very useful to give the latter wide resonance.

For example, on the Facebook page, you can add a dedicated tab that will allow you to build a video clip generated directly from the channel (you can use services like Woobox). On Pinterest, you could create a special board or maybe one for each product, topic, or collaboration you have posted on YouTube.

2. Email Marketing

Sending periodic emails to your subscribers can be very useful to notify you when a new video is released or to bring your attention back to less recent but significant footage.

YouTube does not allow you to send an email notification directly to your subscribers (they are the latter to manage from their profile the ability to receive notifications when favorite channels upload new videos); however, using your site or blog, you can build a database by landing the viewers here and asking them for their email address in exchange for valuable content (such as an e-book, a report, etc.).

3. Video Ads

YouTube video ads are a good opportunity to make yourself known as they allow you to select your target audience based on gender, age, interests, and location. You can choose from among different ad formats the one that best suits your needs.

4. SEO Optimization

There are many practices recommended by YouTube to improve the placement of videos and channels: from the inclusion of keywords in the title and description, to the use of subtitles, until the creation of playlists.

5. Connect the Channel to Site and/or Blog

If your activity involves the use of a website or a blog, it may be useful to insert links to the YouTube channel (provided that it is here that you want to get users and this operation does not risk cannibalizing visits to your site main).

Creating a custom button is very simple, thanks to the easy-to-understand configurator that YouTube makes available.

Embed the videos inside the pages or insert the subscription button.

6. Collaborations

The collaborative videos are born from the work of two or more YouTubers: we find examples in which the creatives find themselves in the same recording space and others where, instead, what we see is the result of the editing of two clips generated in different times and spaces.

Whatever the way they are created, this kind of footage increases exponentially the potential channel of visibility of a channel (as long as the public are similar and have similar interests) and proves useful not only for the personal branding of a Creator: even brands can profitably collaborate with "YouTube stars", reinventing the concept of endorsement to create quality content and relevant to their audience.

7. Fan Search

This is a free channel promotion service offered by YouTube. Each channel will be able to promote itself by creating a pre-roll announcement: the users to whom it will be shown will be the ones that will most closely approach a detailed profile built on the basis of precise interests.

Each video of the channel can be chosen for this type of announcement, even if the trailer is probably the most suitable for this purpose.

8.   Google Hangouts

Hangouts is a Google tool that allows users to make video calls and video conferences (up to 15 people connected).

Google Hangouts also offers many benefits to brands and creators. All video conferencing is broadcasted live on your YouTube channel and on Google+, thus expanding the number of people who can (do not actively participate) access to the content. Once the live broadcast is finished, the video recording will automatically be uploaded to the channel, available to anyone who wants to use it.

This is a tool that is certainly useful for presenting new products and content, collaborations, or perhaps to respond to requests from fans.

9.   Connected Channels

YouTube offers channel managers the opportunity to highlight other channels that may be particularly interesting for their audience. Using this tool is a good idea to cross-promote other channels with similar or complementary content to yours or with which collaborate.

In addition to offering content relevant to your audience,

interacting genuinely with other creators will increase the chances of being included in their "Featured Channels" lists.

10. Analytics

The statistical tools of YouTube are a great help to measure the performance of video and to build or reformulate from them an effective video programming strategy. In addition to the number of views, "Like", "I do not like", comments, and shares, you can access other data on your channel regarding display time, traffic sources, and subscriber demographics.

11. Originality of the Contents

Despite the commitment and perseverance in publishing videos, you cannot increase your views and subscribers to YouTube. If you treat a particular topic and do it exactly like others do, why should a person look at yours?

If you really do not have new ideas, you can try to look at some foreign format and get ideas, and then try to create something totally yours.

12. Give a Visual Impact to your Brand

Think of your channel as if it were a brand; it must be something recognizable in any context that is on YouTube or other social networks. You can also think of a flyer or gadget, so wide to the imagination, choosing fonts and colors that they stay well with each other. Look for a style and always remain coherent.

So, you have to choose a cover and use it on all the

channels that you have available, only so users will be able to associate your brand with content over time.

13. Choice of the Topic

There are many generalist YouTube channels, which make videos of various kinds, treating a bit of everything: from news, to sports, cinema, and so on. Many think it could be a useful choice to attract audiences of various sectors, but being very dispersive is quite risky. On YouTube, there are many channels of this kind, so the best solution is to choose only one topic and treat it well because you will become a point of reference in that specific sector over time, with as much success as possible.

THE 3 MISTAKES TO AVOID AT ALL COSTS WHEN IT COMES TO YOUTUBE

When you subscribe to YouTube, you do it with the hope of breaking through and becoming famous, but you have to take into account several factors such as that of huge competition. So being able to get noticed is not as simple as you think.

There are many YouTubers who want to increase YouTube views and subscribers to their channel, but often make mistakes, even trivial, which lead to the opposite result.

1. Not Having a Publishing Program

It is important to have a plan to publish content. There are channels that publish many videos every day, others that are reduced to a couple of years. We are at two extremes that do not bring any kind of benefit.

In fact, uploading too many videos is not good because the subscribers find the home clogged by the contents and many may decide to remove the subscription to the channel, moreover, making such a large number of videos could decrease the quality of content and topics covered.

On the other hand, doing only a couple of videos a year does not help to build the audience and build a network of subscribers because people will forget about the existence of the channel.

The right solution? It's in the middle, like all things. There are no precise numbers. Much depends on the format. The important thing is to never give up quality; the more beautiful the videos are, the more they are appreciated. A couple of weeks could be the right choice.

2. Not Choosing a Convincing and Impactful Name

Many do not give us the right importance, but choosing the name for your YouTube channel is essential because that word will be associated with the project, the face of the creator, and the videos that will be uploaded.

So, before opening a channel, it is good to think carefully about the nickname to be proposed to the potential public, trying to find the word that best summarizes the main topic of your project.

It should be a name that users will remember easily and will immediately associate with the channel when they see a new video uploaded.

3. Having Low-Quality Videos

The quality of the videos is essential if you want the public to appreciate the published content. In fact, one of the main successes is the user experience. You can also make an interesting video but if you do not understand and do not see well, it will not help very.

So, you have to equip yourself with quality equipment. Even a normal HD camera, which has a better resolution, is fine.

How to Monetize YouTube and How to Use It in a Social Media Marketing Strategy

Have you ever wondered how to make money with YouTube through videos posted online? I bet yes. And if you're here now and you're reading this chapter, it's obviously because you have not yet managed to find a satisfactory answer to your question. If things are actually this way, you know that this time you can count on me too. I can, in fact, provide all the explanations of the case and indicate how to collect the money from your online videos.

To answer immediately your question, know that to earn with YouTube the only valid system is advertising, the ones that are shown before the videos or directly on them. But how do you get them? Simple, you have to become a YouTube partner.

Having clarified this point, if you are really interested in learning more and discovering all that you can do to make money with YouTube, I suggest you take a few minutes of free time and concentrate on reading this tutorial. I do not promise that at the end of this chapter you will become a "maharajah"—thanks to your videos posted on the net—but certainly, you will have much clearer ideas on how to earn some money, thanks to the videos posted on the net on the famous Google platform. So, are you ready? Yes? Very well, so we ban the chatter and start.

As I said, to be able to earn on YouTube, it is essential to becoming a partner of the site. To be accepted in the program, you need to have a fair number of views, many videos uploaded to the channel, and do not have to infringe on copyright or the internal rules of YouTube. If you think you have all the credentials, try it. It costs nothing.

To generate considerable gains, it is also necessary to have a considerable audience. Simply put, there are few, very few, those who manage to "live" only on YouTube (intended as advertising revenue). Many more people can make money—thanks to the personal promotion that YouTube—with its vast range of public, allows them to accomplish it. But this is another matter.

TWITTER

Many people ask how to do marketing on Twitter this year and how to exploit this simple (but powerful) social to promote online communication. Because after all, this is Twitter, right? It is a tool to communicate; it is a tool to track your ideas and your online activity.

With Twitter, you can share text and links. You can (try to) increase your blog visits. You can also post visual content, create threads, and answer the questions of your followers. Even if you only have 140 characters available, the combinations are endless.

Many believe that to get good results on Twitter, you just have to tweet to promote their content. In reality, it is not so. Behind a good success on Twitter, there is careful planning of the activities. Those who know this world know it well, but there are rules that everyone should respect to use this social network in the best possible way.

This year, Twitter is going to be an important part of every social media marketing strategy, as there are more and more users on the platform every day. In the next two chapters, you are going to discover some amazing strategy to take your Twitter marketing to the next level.

The basis of Twitter marketing is simple: this social network is made up of conversations, not soliloquies. So, put aside your isolationism: to be able to grasp the results from this social network you have to interact with people. Or better said, you have to create conversations. You must make sure that there is a natural interest around your brand.

Being human, this is the first rule for those who ask me how to do marketing on Twitter. You cannot hope to get many followers (and many shares) if you continue to live under a glass bell and just post promotional content.

On this social network, visual content is important. You can insert images and videos (both from the desktop and the Twitter application itself), you can enrich tweets with GIFs. You can also activate the big or small Twitter Cards that create a preview of the link you've shared.

The second step is even clearer: you have to become useful, you must become a decisive account for your niche and you have to do it following the rules of Twitter algorithm. What is the secret to achieving this goal? I do not believe in secrets, but in good habits. And what I recommend is simple: share what people love and not the contents that are comfortable for you, or at least not only those.

Last step of the path to answer how to do marketing on Twitter: you have to measure your progress. You must have a clear assessment of your successes or failures. You have to understand what has been lucky and what has been caused by careful planning and create new strategies. You must identify new paths. To do this you need the statistics.

Once, it was all very difficult. Today, Twitter offers a complete analytics platform that meets all needs. To access these pages, go to analytics.twitter.com and start browsing through the various sections. Remember that conversations are important and so are the numbers that make the difference, not your feelings on how a certain campaign is going.

On Twitter, there are 3 types of promotion. Let's look at them one by one.

SPONSORED TWEETS

Sponsored Tweets are regular tweets that are promoted by advertisers who want to reach more users to maximize their followers' interaction. When an advertiser pays for a sponsored Twitter, the tweet is shown as "Sponsored".

For the rest, the sponsored tweets are the same as the other tweets and can be retweeted, they can receive Likes and answers.

They can be useful for various reasons: both for those who want to promote a specific action on Twitter and to increase the popularity of their company.

In fact, the sponsored tweet can:

- increase traffic to the website

- share coupons and discounts in the tweet text

- favor the lead generation through the lead generation page

- promote offers and competitions

- expand coverage of content, such as blog posts

- get in touch with influential people and make sure they see the content

- promote awareness in relation to events and product launches

- ask to retweet and get an even wider audience

If a user is not interested in a sponsored tweet, he can delete it by clicking on the remove button that appears as part of the tweet.

SPONSORED ACCOUNTS

Sponsored Accounts are intended to suggest an account that people do not follow yet but may find interesting. Their function is clearly to rapidly increase the number of followers, so they are functional when you want to be more identifiable by people who might be interested in their business.

Thanks to Sponsored Accounts people can:

- increase their sales
- increase the number of their leads
- increase the popularity of the brand
- increase the web traffic

Sponsored Accounts are displayed in different areas of Twitter, such as in the main dashboard, in the "Who to Follow" page, and in the search results. Obviously, they will appear only if a Sponsored Account is considered relevant to the user's interests. Sponsored Accounts will also be shown under the "sponsored" label to distinguish them from naturally recommended accounts.

SPONSORED TREND

Initially, the Sponsored Trends were born as an extension of the Sponsored Tweet but today, they represent a real autonomous product. Through the Sponsored Trends, users can view advertiser promotions at the top of Twitter's Trend Topics. Even the Promoted Trends are indicated with the "sponsored" label and, sometimes, they can also appear in users' histories.

The only difference between a natural trend and a sponsored trend is the label that indicates the sponsorship of the topic. For the rest, you can click on the trend to view all the tweets that contain the #hashtag and you can tweet including the sponsored trend name in a tweet.

Chapter 2:

FACEBOOK ADVERTISING 101

ADWORDS VS. FACEBOOK

This is a question that often inexperienced marketers ask. The answer is always "it depends".

We need to understand what are the goals that we want to achieve with our advertising campaign. It is often fundamental to combine both strategies. It all depends on the type of question: whether this is latent or conscious (or both).

If the goal is to make branding and then stimulate users who do not know us and may be interested (latent demand), the best choice is Facebook Ads, which will allow you, as we will see later, to reach potential customers. You can do this with various types of targeted campaigns and get leads.

Similarly, you can also take advantage of ads on the Google Display Network to reach potential customers by submitting your banners to specific placements.

If users are already looking for your product or service, the right approach is to use Google AdWords by creating ads on the Search Network. In this case, the user is already in a much lower part of the funnel, therefore more inclined to purchase as the user is looking for your product/service.

Obviously, in most cases, we will find both types of

demand and we will have to work on both platforms jointly.

The key is to understand where the user is inside our sales funnel and act accordingly; we will never tire of stressing it.

Going inside, it will be useful to retarget users who have shown interest in the product or service working with both Facebook Ads and AdWords through ads on the display network.

What if we intercept potential customers on Facebook through FB Ads and these, then, look for us on Google but we are not positioned in an organic way (without paying) for that keyword?

Simple. They will click on a competition link. The risk is, therefore, to practically advertise competitors. Understand well then how important it is, in the absence of organic positioning with SEO, that we must also have Google ads on the search network to cover some keywords as well.

Facebook marketing is not so powerful if done alone; it is something that some people see as a disadvantage.

Each Facebook campaign consists of 3 levels and it starts from the campaign level, which consists of one or more ad groups.

As you have just read, for each campaign you create, you will have to choose a goal. This is the real distinctive factor at the campaign level.

At the Ad Group level (Ad Set), you will have to choose the target, the available budget, the publication times, the offer, and the placements.

Going down the hierarchy, at the level of the announcements, you can set the type of announcement (image, video, carousel, etc.), all the texts, the call to action (action button), and the destination links.

As mentioned, the structure is hierarchical, so if you pause (or delete) for example a group of ads, the same thing will happen to all ads below that group.

THE DEFINITION OF THE GOALS

Now that we understand the structure of a Facebook campaign and what are the parameters to be set for each level, we are ready to launch our first campaign.

The first question is: "What is the goal to be achieved?"

Do you want to sell a certain product because maybe you have an e-commerce store? Do you want to create awareness or reputation? Do you want to have leads?

Often, in a complete web marketing strategy, we will have to create different campaigns for the different phases of the purchasing process. We can then create different ads depending on whether the target user does not know our brand or knows it but does not know our product/service, or, for example, knows our product/service and may be interested in a commercial offer.

Facebook itself in the creation phase will propose you different objectives divided into 4 macro-categories. Let's see them in detail one by one.

- **Brand Awareness**

When to use it: in large-scale campaigns, when there is not a particular action that you want to take to the user. This goal will be more attractive to large companies that can afford to launch campaigns for pure branding. For smaller companies, however, almost every other objective will give better and more significant results.

- **Reach**

When to use it: similar to the brand awareness goal, the reach objective is functional to reach the maximum number of users to which the ad will show. With the introduction of the rules, Facebook now allows you to put a cap on the frequency with which the ad is shown to the same user; in this sense, the goal for reach becomes very useful when you have to work with a relatively small audience and you want everyone to view the ad.

- **Traffic**

When to use it: when we want to take users to a website, or on a landing page, for example. It is a very interesting goal when promoting content, such as a blog post.

- **Leads**

When to use it: the lead ads greatly simplify the signup process from mobile devices. When someone clicks on the ad, a form opens with all personal contact information already pre-filled based on the information they share on Facebook, such as name, surname, phone, and email address. This aspect makes the process really fast and within 2 clicks, one to open the ad and one to send the information.

The only problem with this type of objective is that, often, the email address used to sign up for Facebook several years ago is obsolete and has not been updated for too long. In this case, we would get a useless contact. As a result, it has been seen that better conversion campaigns perform that point to specific external landing pages with data to be filled out.

Another aspect to keep in mind is that lead ads do not allow you to include all the information you want in the offer, like on a landing page. Therefore, for campaigns that require a great deal of cognitive attention from the user, a campaign for conversions will be more successful.

That said, in any case, it is always better to do a test between the two approaches and see which performs better, because each case and sector can behave differently.

The success of a Facebook campaign depends almost entirely on how we select the right target. Good results are not obtained by trying to guess the interests, but only by experimenting and testing, and knowing the right tools.

1. The Pixel of Facebook

James Fend, a Facebook expert, is categorical: the pixel of Facebook should always be installed anyway, even if at the moment, we are not interested in campaigning and even if we believe we do not need anything. But why? Because when it is installed (by entering a code on our website), it starts recording data. The pixel will then be able to make us reach users who come into contact with our site, and these users can be used in future for our listings. It must be installed "regardless" because we may regret not having collected the data when these will help us.

2. Spy on Competitors' Sponsorships

Coming into an advertisement published by our competitors can be a golden opportunity: we can "spy" the target they have chosen for their sponsorship. Just click on "Why do I view this ad?", where the magic is accomplished: we will see exactly what target has set our competitor.

If the interests that our competitor has selected work we do not know, we can get an idea based on the vanity metrics. And in any case, we now have some tools to test.

3. Create a Personalized Audience

Facebook gives us many options to intercept our potential customers and we should always start from our customers or our traffic. For example, we can upload a file with our LinkedIn contacts or newsletter subscribers. We can take advantage of the pixel and select who visits specific pages of the site or generate events (such as sales or add to cart), who spends more time on the site or who visit him more often, or who opens the newsletter.

4. Take Advantage of Other Channels, like AdWords

The ads on Facebook certainly do not answer to any conscious question: we launch the bait to a potentially interested public and hope that someone will realize that they need our product or service. With ads on AdWords instead, we intercept the conscious need: the user need the tires and search on Google, find our ad, and land on our site.

Well, we can take advantage of the results obtained from AdWords. Such as? Just leave the pixel of Facebook "listening" and with the data obtained create our custom audience based on traffic on the site.

At that point the user, who has seen our model X of tires but who has not completed the purchase, will see "chased" from our product even within Facebook.

5. Use A/B Testing

The analysis of the results obtained must always be exploited to our advantage. Facebook gives us the opportunity with A/B testing.

FACEBOOK CAMPAIGNS: RULES TO DEFINE THE BUDGET

The risk of wasting money on Facebook campaigns is very high. To avoid spending money badly, there are a series of precautions that is best to undertake.

Rules to improve CPAs (cost per action) by working on the budget:

Do not choose too ambitious self-optimization goals. This is especially true for e-commerce, but it is always applicable: it takes an amount of daily conversions high enough for campaigns to be able to learn effectively and improve their performance. We use micro-conversions, i.e. intermediate conversions that are easier to obtain.

Head different configurations. When the available budget allows it and "we are allowed to make mistakes", it is good to test different configurations in order to find the ideal setting.

Increase the budget progressively. When a campaign proves to be performing it is normal to want to increase the budget allocated to it and make it climb. However, the increase must be progressive and for small steps (10%-20%). Or, if there is urgency, better clone the campaign and create a new one with the desired budget. Otherwise, 9/10, there is an increase in CPC and a general decline in performance.

Do not accept default placements. Always separate positions in groups with the same target until proven otherwise.

FACEBOOK LEADS: HOW TO GET QUALITY LEADS

Do not stop at the lead. Look for the quality of the contact. Landing pages generate higher quality contacts because they intercept the aware questions and require the commitment to fill out the forms, and the quality is paid (with CPL, costs per lead, high).

The Facebook lead ads have unparalleled CPLs, but the quality is affected. The Facebook form is pre-filled with the user's data and often the latter submits without giving weight to the action, perhaps even just out of curiosity. That's why with the ads, you should never use insertions and forms that are too simple.

Indeed, complex forms, in which we challenge the user with questions (or even propose a quiz) can have a considerable engagement.

Among the various platforms in which to start implementing social media marketing activities, Facebook tends to be one that best meets the marketing objectives of a company.

Numbers are important, but not all count in the same way.

The data have no value in itself; they only have it if they are functional to trigger processes of understanding and improvement of our actions. When it comes to analyzing the activities undertaken on social networks and making reports to understand how it is going, between Internal Insights and External Tools, the feeling is sometimes to get lost in counting and not being able to get some useful information to act better. Today, we see which values should be kept under control with the Insights that Facebook gives us for free.

So let's go to the point.

What are the most important Facebook Insight metrics? Obviously, it depends. It depends on the objectives and KPIs we have set ourselves.

From Facebook Insight, these are the categories available to us:

- **OVERVIEW: The Overview**

In the overview, we immediately realize the progress of our activities in the last week and three fundamental values for the algorithm of Facebook: Like, Cover, and Engagement.

We have a general overview of the volume of Like, the

Coverage achieved by our posts, and the Engagement generated with our activities on the Page.

From the "Export" button, at the top right, in the same bar where we find the Insights, Facebook provides us with quarterly data, exportable in an Excel file.

- **VOLUMES: Like and Post Coverage**

In the Like and Reach section, we provide quantitative information that allows us to monitor fan growth and coverage of our posts.

To understand what percentage of fans actually reached in the Post -> All types of posts section you can view the percentage of posts in percentage, split between Fans/Non-Fans, passing over the mouse pointer.

- **FEEDBACK: The Much Loved (and Feared) Interaction**

For every published post that is a link, a photo or a video or simply text, our desire is always the same: to engage the fans. Recently, Facebook has updated the algorithm inserting as a metric of evaluation of the interest aroused, the time spent to visualize content, even if not explicitly interacting. We do not know how this variable will affect the trend of the pages, but if it were inserted in the Insights, it could become another important value to keep under control.

For now, in the section Posts -> All post published, we can see in percentage what is the rate of involvement by type of post, very useful to understand what kind of content you like most to our fans. Just flag the

Engagement Rate option, as shown in the screenshot below.

The rate of involvement does not express qualitatively what kind of involvement it is and, on the Web, you know, it does not work "as long as you talk about it".

This data should be associated with the Sentiment analysis, which involves a search for specific user-generated content and detects whether the engagement is positive or negative.

In the Reach/Like section, we have an overview of the negative feedback:

- Hide post
- Hide all posts
- Report as Spam
- I do not like it anymore

This type of information is not to be ignored, as it is often done for "unpleasant" feedback. On the contrary, they are very useful to understand how our work is going. But what we are interested in knowing, in particular, is what kind of content has generated negative actions. To understand this, we have to go to the Posts section and flag the hidden posts, hide all the posts, and then report as spam.

- **TIME: Tell Me How Long**

And now we come to a question that cyclically comes back to haunt the Social Media Manager: when is it better to publish?

To answer this question, Facebook gives us a screen with the times in which our fans are online. Here, online does not mean that they are on our page or when they usually display our posts; they are simply on Facebook. The question of the best time to publish is somewhat controversial.

To understand when it is better to publish our posts, we can only test, test, and test. We plan the types of content and test the success, keeping the typology but changing the time of publication, we repeat the tests over and over again, and we will have more concrete indications on the real online presence of our audience.

- **COMPETITOR: See How Good Others Are**

Once the metrics have been identified (fan growth, fans/non-fans coverage, engagement by type of posts, negative feedback, and publication time), we must also keep them under control for our competitors.

Facebook gives us the opportunity to follow 5 competitor pages and watch how they perform. If you're wondering, yes, the competitor page administrator will be notified once the Page is added to the "Page to watch".

The production of content for Facebook goes hand-in-hand with the constant analysis of our performances. Let's not forget to spend some time studying Analytics, the best creative ideas can often come from there!

Let's face it, the best way to achieve important results in the e-commerce world (and not only) is to combine the theoretical and practical study with an analysis of real cases.

Chapter 3:

THE IMPORTANCE OF A FACEBOOK PAGE

S mall and medium-sized businesses (SMEs) can use Facebook marketing strategies with high margins of success. In fact, with more than 2 billion active users every month, it is impossible to remove the blue social from your web marketing plan.

What Could Be the Goals of Facebook Marketing Referring to SMEs?

1. Brand Awareness

Facebook is a very important tool that enables SMEs to make their products and services known, while at the same time cultivating a very direct relationship with interested users.

If on the one hand, your community that is made up of people who already know your products, can follow us on the blue social, then, on the other side, it is possible to reach people who do not know us through spontaneous sharing or through sponsored ones. The latter, through the creation of the right audience, allows reaching to new people potentially interested in our products.

2. Customer Care

Facebook is also one of the websites that best lend themselves to customer care, which is assistance to its customers. Indeed, given the announcement of future updates of the algorithm of the views of the News Feed, focus on customer care could also prove successful in terms of awarding the content posted.

Promotional content can still be valid, but using your own social page as a place to solve problems and perplexities of its users can be a key to use highly because it can trigger conversations between friends, debates, and an engagement appreciated by Facebook algorithms.

3. **Direct Sales**

Facebook can also be used to sell your products or services. Like an e-commerce site, the platform lends itself to the possibility of direct purchase from the page, with huge benefits for users. For SMEs, this opportunity is an important resource for saving resources that would otherwise have to be spent on the creation and management of an entire site.

Obviously, it must be said that those who hold an important business cannot simply rely on the social network of Zuckerberg to market their products online, but it is a fact that not a month passes in which the Menlo Park team does not make availability of some new function that favors those who want to sell via the web.

How to Create a Facebook Marketing Strategy That Works?

Before starting to take action on Facebook, it is good for SMEs to devote time to creating a well-designed communication plan.

First of all, the goals of the strategies to be put in place must be defined.

Secondly, the public must be identified, that is the buyer, the typical customer, tracing a sort of identikit of its main characteristics such as age, place of residence, interests, level of education, and more (see Chapter 6 for more information about this topic).

As for the content, it will be good to dedicate only 20% of them to the promotion of your products or services, so as not to tire the user with continuous offers and hype.

Finally, the tools for checking the results must not be forgotten, with the choice of the most appropriate metrics to follow in order to understand the effectiveness of the steps taken along the road to achieving the designated objectives. For example, if the setting up of a valid customer care campaign has been done, one of the ways to evaluate the effectiveness of the actions carried out is the analysis of the number and quality of comments received, rather than that of 'likes'.

FACEBOOK FOR SMALL BUSINESSES

Why should you use Facebook to market your small business?

Facebook is about to touch the ceiling of a billion users according to the latest official data released in July 2018. The people who connect to this social network are 955 every month and 552 million every day; more than half a billion, even the number of monthly users who connect to Facebook with a mobile device—mobile phone, smartphone, tablet.

Facebook is becoming, for many, a major source of information more and more often, instead of connecting to the homepage of newspapers to see what is happening. We scroll the dashboard reading and commenting on the news linked by our friends. The 2011 CENSIS report on the American company shows that Facebook is used as a source of information by 26.8% of Americans, a percentage that grows to 61.5% in the age group of 14 to 29 years.

The quantity and nature of our relationships have been radically changed by the possibility of keeping in touch with people we do not see daily in person, but for the most diverse circumstances, we feel close. They were our friends in the past, we shared a travel experience or study, or we met online and subsequently met live.

This allows us to listen and exchange opinions, information, points of view, and emotions in this impetuous dynamic of conversations. This is an always open bar where people pass from one group to another participating in dozens of discussions. The companies suddenly find themselves "degraded" to one voice among others, which must gain attention, thanks to the importance of what it says without the possibility of massively occupying the spaces of visibility. Furthermore, we must learn to speak "with" people, which mean, first of all, to listen and respond.

Should your company/association/electoral committee/theater company/excitement have a presence on Facebook? In the vast majority of cases, the answer is yes. Do not fall into the trap of thinking that Facebook is exclusively the realm of lazy people; often times, it is a great way to "feel the pulse" of your stakeholders and can intercept your needs and opportunities that otherwise you would not have known.

In addition, your site is may be where people go once in a while or never go back, but on the contrary, many of them open Facebook every day, several times a day. And if they find what you publish to be interesting enough for them to click on "like" or leave a comment, this makes you visible on the bulletin board of their friends, not in the anonymous way of a flyer tucked in the mailbox, but with the social support of word of mouth.

An effective presence on Facebook can help you:

- Increase your visibility, spreading the posts of your blog, the videos you shoot, and the photos you take

- Establish a more intense relationship with your customers, better knowing their needs, and obtaining important feedback on what you do

- Motivate and gratify your "super fans"

- Promote and share initiatives, special offers, and new products

A Facebook group is a micro-community within the largest community of the network that, focusing on specific themes, attracts people to the target.

To this, we add that the groups have recently had the blessing of Facebook after the hard blow to the business pages in the latest updates of the EdgeRank algorithm.

What happened to the Facebook algorithm?

The turning point came with the announcement of Zuckerberg and the subsequent official confirmation on the blog of Facebook news. In fact, the Newsroom informs users of an epochal change: less visibility on the pages in favor of a more personal communication.

More visibility for the posts of friends and family, but also explicitly mentioned by Zuckerberg, to the groups.

Unlike pages, in fact, groups have a greater predisposition to the generation of discussions and not to the simple unilateral posting of content. Precisely, this content— with little interaction—is the one against which Facebook wants to fight. The decision comes after the progressive descent of the engagement on the posts that are over the years has characterized the Social Network of Menlo Park.

What does this mean? It simply means that the posts on the groups will have greater visibility and the possibility to reach more easily your target audience. It seems to me, therefore, an excellent idea not to neglect them.

How to Find Facebook Groups in Target

Let us imagine, of course, that you have already identified the niche or sector on which to base your communication strategy. The first of the problems you need to solve is to find groups to distribute your content on. Let me show you a couple of techniques you can use.

1. *Facebook Searches*

If you have an active Facebook account in America, you can use the search bar to find groups that meet your requirements. For example, if you look for a group that deals with social, you can write "social media" on the search bar and then apply the filter "groups" (Facebook will initially search among posts, people, and so on).

If you want to get even smarter, I recommend you to use Facebook in English. You will open other very interesting possibilities! Facebook in English supports the "Graph Search", thanks to which it is possible to create more complex searches such as: "Groups joined by my friends who like social media". That is, look for groups to which were added by part of my friends who like social media.

Or you might still be looking for users who like certain pages or groups in an area of interest. For example: "Friends who like Wired". You can then go to peek at the groups in which your friends have entered, going directly to their profile (privacy permitting!).

2. *Use Facebook Tips*

Of one thing we can be extremely sure of is that Facebook knows us more than we think! It is for this reason that it will be easy for them to suggest groups that might be interesting to you based on the past history of your likes and the groups in which you are already inside.

Just go to the Facebook page dedicated to groups. On the upper part of the drop-down menu, you can enter the "Discover" tab. Here, you will find lots of suggestions divided by categories, including the "local" one to find geographically close groups.

This feature is available on both desktop and mobile. In the latter case, you will go to the main menu> Groups> Suggested.

I remind you that the specific features of the groups were recently incorporated into the main app of Facebook, while the app "Facebook Groups" retired in September 2017.

WHAT TO DO BEFORE POSTING CONTENT IN GROUPS

I already know that you're cheating to publish your content on the groups of your interest, but before starting to spam I suggest you follow some rules.

1. *Always look carefully at group usage policies.*

Any self-respecting group manager sets up rules in their own group to prevent the occurrence of phenomena such as spam, excesses of OT (Off Topic, i.e. ending off the arguments to which the group is dedicated), too much promotion, trolling, and so on.

This means that there may be rules on the amount of content that can be submitted to the community, for example. Or that you can publish external links to Facebook only with the permission of the admin.

Policies are often indicated in the first post above, often attached with a "pin". Or they could be in the "file" section of the group. Study these rules well and behave accordingly.

2. *Keep to general rules of good behavior.*

Apart from the policies, which rightly dictate contents,

times, and rhythms, there are also rules of good common life that should always be respected. If you produce content in large quantities:

- Do not spam it all the time.

- Always check that it is in theme with the group, that they are of quality, and that they can be useful and relevant.

- If possible, add a note to the article, a textual status that, for example, highlights a sentence of the article or that poses a question capable of generating a valuable discussion.

Remember, these are not only your contents! Subscribe to the groups, be in silent mode, and then spam your news as if there is no tomorrow, these will certainly irritate the admin that at some point they might even think to kick you out!

Even more so, later in this historical moment, the use statistics of the group have been made available to the administrators.

My advice is to always balance your content with content from other sources. And it would be desirable to participate in the discussions, in addition to the normal posting!

If you already produce your content and think that it is sufficient for your strategy, it means that you skipped the previous paragraph. Go read it!

For a content strategy, whether linked to the development of your business or to your personal branding, you need news and content about your industry.

I know I'm repetitive, but I'll write it again: *you cannot just talk about yourself!* To find valid content on the web, you can use many tools like the simplest monitoring software (I think of Google Alerts or Talkwalker) or news aggregator sites like Feedly.

In the era of the so-called "content shock", where our ability to absorb information is definitely lower than the amount of content produced, the figure of the creator becomes of primary importance. Skimming the contents and proposing the best to a community, therefore, becomes a primary role.

Facebook Advertising 2019

Chapter 4:

FACEBOOK ADS

Many of you have already experienced what it means to have a product for your hands that you like, have the first sales but do not know, then how to go beyond that limit of saturation that we all know very well.

So, I hope these posts can be useful to turn some of you into a future power seller.

In the post, acronyms are used. If you are new and you have difficulty, here is a little legend of acronyms:

- PPE: Goal Page Post Engagement

- WC: Objective Website Conversion

- WC LC: Website Conversion objective optimized for Link Click

- WC ATC: Target Website Conversion optimized for Add To Cart

- WC P: Website Conversion objective optimized for Purchase

- CA: Custom Audience

- LAL: LookAlike (Similar Audience)

I often start with an EPP and a hot targeting: fans of my page, friends of the fans intersected with a broad interest (after speaking in person with one of the Smartly (smart.ly) engineers are less and less inclined to intersections but in some cases I still use them), CA on ATC events (Add to Cart) or Purchase related to the account, etc.

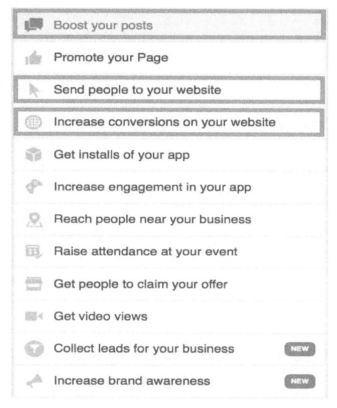

I use the EPP as an "entry" (in this screenshot you only see the WC) because I try to always create engagement around a new product even if I already know the niche and often risk not to go in ROI in this first phase.

Remember that the auction mechanism on Facebook is based on 2 main factors: your bid + engagement.

For this reason even today, I prefer to move like this:

PPE -> WC LC -> WC ATC -> WC P

I do not change what wins for subsequent optimization.

If a WC LC works, I do not go to an ATC WC at most in parallel if the audience is big, but I never close what it sells.

If something does not work or I have a high cost per purchase, I try the subsequent optimizations (duplicating and closing the previous ones). If I do not get anything, I close.

I can work with small or large segments even though as you know by now, I prefer to use large volumes and rely on the algorithm of Facebook.

But since it does not always work, also test to small audiences.

If I'm over 200/300K, I go to Manual Bid, while Auto Bid for small audiences.

Obviously, this is my method and it is not the only one!

Be elastic and put your project at the center more than any advice read in some group (yes, even here).

Use this post (and others) to inspire and think about your project from another point of view.

FEATURES OF A WINNING CAMPAIGN: RETARGETING

Retargeting techniques generate more than 50% of sales.

I use various strategies:

- Retargeting to CA (first two lines): The simplest retargeting of all, the one that I explain in the basic course. Actually, it is based on that principle, but it is structured in such a way as to show different contents after a few days. In this campaign, I segmented CAs over two periods. I have recently started segmenting them in 4 periods. Confused? I promised you a video about this technique but I saw a few people interested.

- Video Retargeting: Oh, this is a technique that I have felt for a long time, and I consider it excellent. It works often and is perfect in all those situations where you have poor initial targeting. Take a video of interest. One of those with a lot of engagement. If you can, edit it in a different way and extrapolate the basic concepts and insert them in a single campaign. Post it to the page and create a Video Views campaign with this post. $3-5 a day for 48 hours or even more if it works. Create a LAL from this audience and start bombarding them with a WC LC, and then WC ATC, and so on.

- Retargeting on page/post interaction: This type of retargeting is working a lot. This strategy is implemented by constantly posting viral content on the page (use PostPlanner) and using the new tools you find in audiences. I often work "People Engaged with post" and usually imposed a window of 60 days. If you have different numbers with other settings, I would love to know your tests on this topic.

- ATC retargeting no purchase: It almost always works.

This is one of the reasons why I open an account for every niche I try to scale massively. Create a CA of the ATCs to which you remove the Purchase. In this way, you make a retargeting on all those who have left the cart. Offer an incentive (discount).

The Secret Weapon: The LookAlike (LAL)

This is really an amazing strategy and I'd love to meet a Facebook engineer to be able to talk with him about it.

The artificial intelligence behind these algorithms is, in my opinion, disconcerting. When I was studying AI at the university, I never thought I could see such applications someday.

How do I start? From LAL 1% on CA visits.

I do it more or less when I see a CA of 50-100. But it is not a rule.

WARNING: It takes patience. They are sets that update every 6 hours depending on the audience's responses to your ads. If you use well, they improve day after day but they need time to improve.

So do not close them right away especially if you see that the engagement improves day after day.

As you have seen, I use the LAL in all sauces (Video, Post/Page Engagement retargeting, and others).

Manage Costs and Increase ROI: Manual Bidding

Well, what about the mechanism that has transformed my way of climbing campaigns? It's quite difficult to explain in this post all the tricks that I use but I'm trying to do it in the group by answering when I can your specific cases.

What I want to do here is to respond to those who are afraid to raise the budget in manual (some of you in these days I had expressed his fear).

Remember that increasing the budget of an adset to $500-$1,000 a day is not the same as spending them all! This happens if you go to Auto Bid, but in manual bidding, things change!

Apart from some retargeting adset, the others are in manual bid and each has about $500 a day budget.

If your fears were founded, this WC campaign would make me spend more $5,000 a day with a return of only 30k.

Clear, use this system only if you know what you're doing.

Facebook Advertising 2019

Chapter 5:

FACEBOOK GROUPS

The group is made up of the most loyal fans, people who believe in your company, in your product, and in your values. Brands like Canva, who has a loyal fan base, called these groups "community groups" or "ambassador groups".

The one with the loyal fans is the most important group you can create on Facebook. It is important to create a positive word of mouth on your products, your company, and your activities. Be sure to make your fans feel special. You can do it in various ways: send them a shirt or put a comment on them.

The most important thing is to thank them, heartily and regularly. A written note (maybe by hand) is much more pleasant than a gift. Thank your fans for helping you grow your community and achieve your goals.

Here are 5 ways you can use these groups:

1. *Get feedback on new products.*

You have a new product to launch but first, you want to know how it would be accepted? This is the right place to test it.

2. *Attract new members.*

If your company has a membership program, this is a great way to keep in touch with them and attract new ones.

3. *Answer the questions.*

How many times have you seen a question on a group or an online forum and have you thought that your product could be the ideal solution? Of course, you could answer the question with your private profile, but you will be more successful by responding to the members of your group.

Answer often to questions and to avoid spam (especially if there are many members in the group), tag two or three experts in the response that can respond appropriately.

4. *Recruit experts.*

Many people like to feel expert and be taken into consideration. And many like to share their knowledge with other people. Experienced people can help new consumers get closer to your product and buy it. Please note that it may be necessary to create a dedicated expert group.

5. *Share the company's achievements.*

If the company wins a prize or is named in an important publication, let the whole world know about it. You can then call your friends, family, post the news on your private profile, but in this way, you will not go very far. If your company receives a prize, share the news with the fan group. That's why Facebook exists.

HELP YOUR CUSTOMERS

The second type of Facebook groups is dedicated to acquired customers. To build this community, invite people to join the group as soon as they make a purchase.

Make customers aware of the existence of the group and that you would like them if they, too, registered.

Explain how the group works in the "information" section, as Golden Tote does. For example, members can get to know each other, share ideas and strategies, and help each other in any way.

Be sure to send an email with the link to subscribe to the group and monitor who signs up or not. Do not forget to invite people who have not yet registered several times.

Ways to develop your group on Facebook:

- *Be generous and promote a "give" policy.*

For example, offer tips or tricks to use the less known features of your product and invite other users to share their findings.

You could invite members of your fan group to share tips and tricks with them too.

- *Be transparent.*

Respond personally to customer criticism. For example, acknowledge the customer who makes you notice what is lacking in your product and responds that you will immediately fix it.

It is not necessary to promise discounts or promotions to the disgruntled customer, but it is important to thank him for the report, to apologize, and to promise that he will be contacted when the problem is solved.

- *Be present.*

Answer questions and comments as soon as possible. If

you cannot give an immediate answer, still let your customer know that you will respond quickly. From suggestions, tips, and tricks. Encourage other users to share their findings.

- *Be inclusive.*

Offer group members promotions and offers that are not on the official page. Make your customers feel part of an exclusive club. If a social media user shows a particular interest in your product, he also invites you to join the online group.

GROW TARGET SEGMENTS (WITH MULTIPLE FACEBOOK GROUPS)

One of the most important goals of marketers is to develop a "typical customer", that is to identify their customers and understand what their doubts, problems, and how your product can meet its needs.

If you have different types of customers, create more groups on Facebook. For example, you could create a group based on the language spoken by its users. Maybe not all customers will want to be considered experts and to answer questions from other users; you can then create smaller groups to meet the needs of each client.

Now that we have seen how Facebook groups can have a profound impact on your social media marketing strategy, it is time to see how to create your very own group. Managing your own Facebook group may seem complicated at first, but will pay off quite a lot in the long run.

Maybe you do not know, but creating a group on Facebook allows you to share photos, videos, and anything else just with whoever you want. Thanks to groups, you can interact with a small circle of people without the others seeing what you're sharing with them.

Even if you do not consider yourself a social network expert, you can feel comfortable. In the next paragraphs, you will find all the information you need to create a Facebook group, whether you intend to act on your PC or your mobile device. In addition, you can find some useful tips for creating group chats on Messenger and use them to share various types of information with friends and relatives. What do you say? Are you ready to start? So, let's put aside the talk and get straight into the heart of this tutorial. I wish you good reading and have fun!

Wanting to create a group on Facebook but unfamiliar with the social network founded by Mark Zuckerberg, you do not have the faintest idea how to proceed? No fear! Just follow the steps listed below to complete the task.

PC

To create a group on Facebook, from your PC, connect by the browser to the website of the social network—of course, after you have already logged-in to your account—and click on the green Create Group button located at the top right.

In the box that opens, type the name you want to assign to the group in the text field located under the entry 'Give a name to the group', select the users you want to include in the latter by typing their names or their email addresses in the field text placed under the entry 'Add some people', and then select one of the privacy settings available to decide who will be able to view the content posted. Select 'Public Group' to allow all users of Facebook to view the group and the content posted in it, 'Group Closed' to allow everyone to find the group and see the members but without being able to view the posts, or 'Secret Group' to allow only members of the group to find it and view its posts.

After choosing the name of the group, the members that will be part of it, and the privacy settings, click on the blue button 'Create', select an icon that identifies the latter (e.g. the icon of the basketball, if your new group is dedicated to the world of basketball or the camera icon, if your group talks about photography) and click on the blue 'OK' button. If you wish, you can also skip this step by clicking on the 'Skip' button.

Once the procedure is complete, you will be sent back to the main page of your group, which you can customize by inserting a cover image. To do so, click on the green 'Upload Photo' button and upload an image saved on your PC or click on the 'Select Photos' button to use an image from those you have already uploaded to your Facebook profile.

To interact with friends who are part of the group, click on 'Post to Write a New Post', click on the item 'Add Photo/Video' to insert a multimedia content or on the voice 'Live Video' to start a live broadcast with other members of the group.

After creating the group, click on the options that are

located immediately below the name of the group (top left); "Information", to add a description to the group; "Discussion", to share content with other members; "Members", to view members who are part of the group and to modify their roles; "Events", to create an event on the group or "Manage the Group", to create scheduled posts, accept subscription requests, view the activities of administrators, and so on.

To change other settings concerning the new Facebook group you have created, click the 'More' button (after clicking on the 'Discussion' option) and, in the menu that appears, click on one of the options you see: "Add Members", to add new members to the group or "Edit Group Settings", to change their name, select the group type (that is, the category related to the topic dealt with in the same), link a page, select who can publish a post, and so on.

ANDROID

To create a group on Facebook from your Android device, first, start the official social network app on your smartphone or tablet and log in to your account (if required). Then, tap on the symbol ($\equiv$) located at the top right, press the 'Create Group' button (located under the heading Groups), type the name of the group in the text field 'Give a name to this Group' and, if you wish, press on the camera symbol to take or add a photo.

Then, add the members to be included in the group by selecting them from the menu located at the bottom of the screen and press the 'Next' button. At this point, select the privacy settings by ticking one of the available options:

"Public", to create a public group and then allow anyone to view the posts and members that are part of it; "Closed", to hide the posts published on the group to those who are not members or "Private", to make the group "invisible" to those who are not part of it. After indicating the privacy options you prefer the most, press on the item 'Create'. Et voilà! You've just created your group on Facebook!

Even on Android you can add new members, edit group info, create events, post photos, files, and anything else using the appropriate commands that you find immediately under the name that identifies the group.

Ios

To create a group on Facebook from your iOS device, start the Facebook application, log in to your account (if necessary), press the symbol ($\equiv$) located at the bottom right and then tap on the item 'Groups'. In the screen that opens, press the symbol (+) located at the top right, type the name of the group in the text field 'Give a name to this group' and, if you wish, press the symbol of the camera to shoot or add a photo to be used as a cover for the group.

Now, choose the members to add to the group by selecting them from the menu at the bottom and press the 'Next' button. Then, select the privacy settings by ticking one of the available options: "Public", to create a public group; "Closed", to hide the posts published on the group to those who are not part of it or "Private", to not allow those who are not members of the group to find it, nor to display the posts. Finally, press the item "Create" to complete the group creation procedure.

Now, you can finally customize your new group, add new members, edit the info, post photos, and anything else using the buttons that are immediately below the name and photo of the group itself.

CREATE A CHAT GROUP ALONG WITH YOUR GROUP

If your intention is simply to converse with other Facebook users, you probably do not need to create real Facebook groups, but you can simply create simple group chats using the appropriate feature included in Messenger.

- To create a group chat on PC, log in to your Facebook account from the browser, click on the "Messenger" icon (the lightning bolt symbol at the top), click on the item "New group", type the name of the group chat in the text field "Assign a name to the group", select the users to add to the chat and click the blue "Create" button.

- To create a group chat on smartphones and tablets, however, start the Messenger app on your device, press on the voice "Groups", tap on the item "New Group" (on Android) or "Create" (on iOS) and finally press on an 'arrow symbol' (on Android) or on the "Create Group Entry" (on iOS) to complete the operation.

When discussing Social Media as an engine for the growth

of an online business and specifically Facebook Marketing, we tend to think about Fan Pages and how to exploit them to make brand awareness and generate web traffic.

In reality, on Facebook, there is another very powerful tool and in some cases even more effective than the fan pages. We are talking about Facebook Groups.

Although it may seem a lot less "cool", a successful Facebook Group can be a very interesting channel for acquiring web traffic.

In this chapter, we will discuss some very useful tips to quickly grow a Facebook Group.

Before entering into the heart of this topic, I would like to make a small premise.

As you may already know, a new business begins to achieve extraordinary results when it manages to create around itself a community of similar people with shared interests.

By dealing with digital projects, our focus will be moving towards a specific type of community: the online community, the concept that is right behind a Facebook group.

ANATOMY OF AN ONLINE COMMUNITY

Generally, an online community consists of three distinct categories of users:

- 90% are lurkers in public;

- 9% is the average contributors; and

- 1% is loyalists.

By lurker, we mean all those users who hide among the members of a community and who observe, read, and use the information shared by the group, but without them going to interact and feed the conversation.

Why do they behave this way? Maybe because they believe they are not up to certain discussions, perhaps because they are shy people even in digital or because active participation still entails a waste of energy and time to devote to the online conversation.

Then, there is the average contributor, those who together make up 9% of the community and who share useful contents from time to time with a variable frequency.

Lastly, there is the hardcore of the online community, 1% of the "Highlander" or, rather, the loyalists. They are the ones who check every day the postings spread in the group, ask questions, provide feedback to other users, and that would continue to feed the conversation in the group if it were not that at some point of the day, you still have to eat and sleep!

WHY SHOULD WE FOCUS ON THE ONLINE COMMUNITY OF A FACEBOOK GROUP?

One of the greatest benefits of developing a community on Facebook is the concept of target reach.

It is well known that a post published on a Facebook page organically reaches only a very small part of the fans of that page, while, if you post the same content on a Facebook group, such sharing will be notified to every single member of the community.

So, the coverage of a post is far higher within a Facebook group and therefore also all actions related to it.

It is a very useful tool to generate web traffic for a company or personal site. But to be really effective, it must be based on interesting metrics; the first of all is certainly the number of participating members.

I would, therefore, like to share some very useful tips to quickly grow the user base of a successful Facebook group.

1. *Perform a preliminary analysis.*

First, you need to ask yourself what the topics are and these will be the subject of discussion of the group you want to develop.

As a result, you will be able to outline a profile of your ideal target. You cannot aim to have anyone enrolled in your Facebook community; you have to aim for the right people.

Ask yourself what your group is about. This will also be the answer concerning who really is your ideal target and what are its main characteristics.

For more profiling, you can always make sure that the members themselves define themselves better. Create market research in which you try to extrapolate more or less information about the people themselves.

2. *Set goals.*

Once you have a clear idea of the context on which your group revolves, it's time to think about what goal you want to pursue thanks to the Facebook group.

Do you do it for personal interests than for your brand? Why do you like networking with professionals like you? Or why do you simply want to create a community of people available to each other?

Whatever your goal is, having defined it will help you adapt each situation to pursue the search results.

3. *Set it up the right way.*

A successful Facebook group cannot ignore, first of all, an effective name, which is as simple as it is attractive and which can arouse curiosity and interest.

Also, think about any keywords that may be useful for searches on the internal Facebook engine.

About keywords, on the sidebar of a Facebook group or in the general settings (which you can access by clicking on the three points on the top right, near the cover image), you find a field where you can define up to 3 tags, useful for being able to be found by people.

For proper setup, take into consideration the clear description that explains what topics are treated in the group and what kind of people are registered.

In addition, you will also have to decide whether to set the group as closed, public or secret.

Starting from the last just mentioned, a secret group can be found on Facebook only by its members while a public group allows anyone, even those who are not part of the community, to see the posts shared within it.

The most effective type to quickly acquire new members

in the Facebook group is the closed one. A closed group can be found by any user during a search on Facebook using the appropriate keywords, but only members can see the content published in it.

Therefore, those who are really interested in consulting what is within the group must first register. This could be an interesting profiling process though, so think about it before deciding whether to create a public or secret group.

4. *Define the rules.*

A healthy relationship, even the virtual one, between people must be based on clear and precise rules. Without the guidelines, anarchy would reign and anyone could do what they like. For example, you could only share links related to your site, constantly spamming, and you could respond in the comments using unpolished tones.

This could cause serious damage to the image of the group, difficult to repair in a short time.

In addition to this set of rules, which in digital jargon is called netiquette, you must also know how to handle cases in which heated discussions are developed between the various members.

Therefore, we must intervene, bring order, and try to make sure that members can return to converse with calm tones. It is the so-called crisis management.

If, in the case, certain unpleasant situations persist, such as the continuous sharing of posts related to personal services, these articles should be removed. The responsible person should be warned and possibly banned should he repeat this behavior several times.

5. *Share useful content.*

Doing Content Marketing is essential everywhere on the web, let alone in a successful Facebook group.

If you do not share valuable content, you do not feed the discussion among the members, and in that absence, there are no reasons for having to be part of an online community.

So it is essential to design an editorial plan for your Facebook group, both in terms of content creation (creation of original content) and content curation (sharing of useful material created by other people).

In addition, if you want to optimize your work, you can always use one of the various digital tools available for post-programming on a Facebook group. For example, you could try PostPickr; it is a very useful tool that can help you take your business to the next level.

To increase the acquisition of new members and, above all, increase the engagement of those already present, as the group's admin, you have to publish with a certain regularity, perhaps even including questions in the texts of the posts to fuel a constructive debate between the people.

It could be once a day, twice a day, or even less, such as 2-3 times a week.

The important thing is that you understand one thing: you have to offer quality content that can really arouse interest and be useful to your subscribers.

Also, remember two other interesting features of Facebook groups:

- You can highlight a post compared to the others (the "Pin the Post" feature). For example, if you find that a content can prove to be of absolute value for all members or if you want to keep the rules of the community easy to consult.

- In addition to publishing links, you can also upload files (for example, a pdf file), conduct surveys, direct live events, organize events, and create documents linked to the group.

    6. *Shape your team.*

In the beginning, when the group consists of a few tens or hundreds of members, it will not be necessary to have other collaborators to manage the community.

But when you start having thousands of participants, the situation could get out of hand: too many requests for registration links sharing of dubious usefulness, colored verbal exchanges between members, etc.

A simple remedy is to ask for help from other people. In short, set up a team of admin and moderators of the group.

Both these figures can:

- Approve or deny access to the group

- Approve or deny the publication of a post

- Remove posts and comments

- Remove and ban members

- Highlight a post

The substantial difference that exists between an administrator of a group and a moderator is that the former can offer and remove the role of admin or moderator to other members and can make changes to the general settings of the group (name, cover photo, privacy level, etc.).

7. *Promote the group.*

If your tactics for organic and natural growth are tight and you want to take advantage of other techniques to quickly increase the number of members of your community, I suggest you try the following strategies.

First of all, you could start Facebook advertising campaigns to reach new people potentially interested in your group.

The Facebook Ads do not allow you to create a post natively sponsored for the promotion of a group, but there is a simple trick to turn the obstacle.

So, what you can do is create a Facebook page related to your group, create an advertisement linked to it, and enter the URL address of your Facebook group in the field associated with the website to be sponsored.

In this way, people will be conveyed directly to your online community and, if they are really interested in the topics you have proposed, they will not hesitate to register.

Another possibility to increase the number of members is represented by cross-promotions. It is about making new collaborations with other Facebook groups more or less related to the issues faced by your community. The purpose of this collaboration is based on the exchange of promotions between groups; just publish the URL address of the partner group and invite their members to follow the other group, if they consider it appropriate.

Chapter 6:

COMMON MISTAKES AND HOW TO AVOID THEM

COMMON MISTAKES FOR BEGINNERS

The main reason is represented by an imposing and transversal critical mass (over 122 million users in America) that is unmatched in any other social network, within which a large part of its potential audience is likely to be present.

If we add to this a very low access threshold (you can monetize already sustained media investments such as photos, articles, videos, etc.) and some interesting advertising possibilities, it becomes easy to see how the Californian colossus has become one of the favorite platforms of Worldwide.

Precisely with the advantages listed, however, planning an editorial activity on a corporate Facebook page can become a source of clamorous mistakes, misunderstandings with its customers and gaffes that are difficult to remedy, capable of shaking even the most authoritative brands.

In this chapter, we list some of the major mistakes that any brand about to start a business on Facebook should keep in mind, and try to avoid.

1. *Not having a strategy*

People's own content page is an activity that, to bring concrete results, must be programmed with accuracy, according to criteria of efficiency (e.g. availability of multimedia material) and effectiveness (e.g. contents that stimulate the involvement of users), creating the mix that best lends itself to stimulate your audience and reach the set goals.

Basing its presence solely on the dissemination of commercial content, for example, with repeated links to product/service pages, is one of the temptations in which it is not only easier to fall, but which only results in the early loss of interest in comparison of the brand by their fans.

2. *Not having defined goals*

Improvisation is, in particular, in the field of social media marketing, one of the mistakes most often made by companies, often because of the apparent ease of use of many platforms and/or tools.

This rule also applies to Facebook: approaching the platform without having considered the most appropriate strategy to follow and without having first defined clear, specific, and measurable objectives to pursue. It means starting an activity that will be completely the same, if not counterproductive.

3. *Not having a posting schedule*

Finding the right timing to publish your updates is an essential element to determine your visibility on Facebook. Understanding the most correct frequency certainly requires some time (and attempts), since it varies according to the relevant public (there is no rule applicable to all).

In this way, however, we will be able to maximize the

visibility of our posts, avoiding too large editorial "holes" or, on the contrary, of clogging the Home Page of our contacts with too close updates with the risk of losing the acquired fans and coming "hidden" from the respective news flows.

COMMON MISTAKES FOR INTERMEDIATES

When you are an intermediate Facebook marketer, there are two main mistakes that you risk to make. Correcting them as soon as possible is the first step to get to the next level.

1. *Do not remember the balance between performance and results.*

I find that mentally splitting the campaign objectives between performance and results is the most effective starting point.

Remember? In Facebook, "performance" is all that at the campaign level aims to increase the yield in terms of Likes, Comments, Shares, and Reproductions of content that live on the social. On the other hand, "results" goes to cover all those campaigns that aim to bring the user on the site and monitor, possibly, conversions.

This is the enormous strength of Facebook: being able to tap into a social context to direct people to an external site or vice versa.

Thus, some of the questions to be asked become: when do I need to track the performance of a Facebook content? When do I need to track results, in terms of leads collected on a landing?

In this sense, collecting Likes for a brand page becomes just a piece of the puzzle. A campaign with this goal is just the first step to deliver a targeted editorial strategy to this fan base. Or, maybe use this audience in a second campaign, this time with the goal "Address people to your website". Or, you can develop a similar audience again.

In the same way, increasing the visualizations of a video allows you to think first of the performance (the reproductions obtained, of course) and on a horizon to results, building a list of audiences based precisely on the percentages of reproduction.

Before thinking about ad creativity, mentally divide the opportunities given by Facebook in terms of performance and results is the best (and really strategic) way to proceed.

2. *Ignore the new features*

One of the best adjectives to describe Facebook Ads is "seething". In eternal modification and improvement, new features are screaming loudly, especially among industry professionals. In other cases, they pass undertone or are released in installments without precise timing.

Taking advantage of the opportunities offered by any new ad setup or bidding mechanics is especially important when it comes to refinements that are still young, of which we do not know any future, but that could bring interesting results. Arriving first, in this case, is an opportunity not to be missed.

COMMON MISTAKES FOR ADVANCED FACEBOOK MARKETERS

1. *Not being reactive*

Do not assume that what works today can continue to do so without changes in the coming times. Be ready to push (even at the budget level) what works, seizing the opportunities when they arise.

Come back to your campaigns as often as possible, look at reports critically, and, above all, be ready to change your mind: not always the most creative ad is the one that converts the best. Not always the call to action that you have retouched for a long time is the most effective. The ego has nothing to do with it: you only look at the results.

2. *Not dividing the campaign by placements*

Facebook does its best to give as much exposure as possible to its advertisers' ads. However, this visibility does not always coincide with the best context to make our message effective.

Dividing each campaign at least between desktop and mobile is the basis for avoiding dispersion of the message across multiple fronts. Refine the message between smartphone and tablet is the next step.

With the progressive development of Facebook Ads, it is not uncommon to find campaigns automatically addressed to the news feed on desktop, mobile, tablet, within Instagram, and on the audience network. As much as possible, separate each front with different creativities and approaches, even at the budget level.

Some advice?

The desktop news feed is great for generating engagement, since it supports longer texts and more readable descriptions;

The mobile news feed is more effective to reach a target that does not yet know us, bringing the first click on a landing and allowing us to act in remarketing in the medium term. The right-hand column is always less efficient, but often cheaper and still useful in remarketing contexts;

The audience network is interesting as an opportunity to collect clicks from in-target users, but it is scarcely relevant to point directly to conversions;

The positioning on Instagram is everything to test niche for niche, but, realistically, it can work better on more emotional contexts.

3. *Not testing different creatives and levers*

Not all messages work the same way. Especially when there is not a real campaign historian—or other marketing strategies that can provide a canvas are not active—the real challenge is to grasp which "form" has the ideal announcement for those who receive it.

In this case, experimenting is a must. Head different images with different tones, with or without people inside. Evaluate more or less long texts and the presence or absence of links. Change the call to the action present under the content (if the campaign goal allows it). Different colors with different intensities could bring out or bury your ad regardless of the message.

Do not just offer a single ad and see clicks, conversions, and cost reports arrive. It is not satisfactory. The goal is to understand what is the best cost/result ratio that can be achieved and with which creativity.

Chapter 7:

THE BEST CONTENT TO PUBLISH ON FACEBOOK TO GROW YOUR BUSINESS

The best content on Facebook this year is the one that involves and stimulates communication. There is no single formula to write a successful content, but there are some tricks that can help you increase the effectiveness of your posts:

- Publish posts in the best time. Analyze when your audience is online to optimize your publication time.

- Evaluate your audience. Track the performance of your posts and find out what they like most to your target and what is the winning content for your editorial plan. I will talk shortly about the importance of analytics.

- Take advantage of current issues and trends. Find out what are the topics that infect users using services like Google Trends, trending topic on social media, or follow the calendar of events for your industry (even local ones, if they are relevant to you).

- Use the questions as a call to action to encourage users to leave comments under your own publication.

- Miscellaneous content. The predictability of your posts can damage your strategy: try different types of content, alternating topics and formats of your publications to not bore your audience.

The video format is interesting, not only because Facebook tends to prioritize it, but also because it is the one most loved by users among the various types of content that you can publish on your page.

Here is a small selection of tips for video optimization for Facebook:

- Upload videos directly to Facebook because posts with YouTube links lose visibility (Facebook gives priority to videos uploaded on its platform)

- Ideal format: Facebook recommends using MP4 and MOV, a complete list of recommended formats you can find Facebook recommends uploading videos with a maximum duration of 15 seconds, with attractive and high-quality content.

- The public on Facebook also appreciates long read texts when they are written really well (if the theme is current it is easy to generate conversions): why shouldn't the same rule work for the video?

- Upload the videos with subtitles (about 85 % of videos are shown without the sound) and do not forget to add a title and a small description to make people understand the subject of the video right away.

- Video streaming is another type of content that Facebook likes so much and can get yourself a good organic reach. When you create a Live on

Facebook, all your friends and followers will be notified of the start of a new stream, so everyone can follow and comment on your video live.

Content marketing and content curation are two of the words that most marketers will be interested in this year. Content marketing is a much more extensive approach that is not limited to the Facebook channel but can play a decisive role on the same platform. I speak of the choice and creation of content to be conveyed in their fan page that, if chosen accurately, with an attractive graphics and communicated in the right way (sometimes, even in the right time) can become "viral" going to end even outside of our primary user target. However, by doing so, it could give us the advantage of expanding our brand positioning to other target users, who, until then, though we were not interested in us. Translated into simple words, the content conveyed on the page, through sharing and "like", can attract new users to know our brand and start to follow it from the page.

Facebook insights provide much more data than before and the service is almost similar to Google Analytics. Periodically going to "combing" the data helps to better understand what are the content most appreciated by users and those that generate greater shares (now, we can also know what are the comments with "sentiment" negative, even if the service is not very reliable). From the analysis of our pages and those of our customers, it appears that quality images (especially those released for the first time and then created in house) and videos (in second place) are those that reach the best level of engagement (likes, shares, and comments), and, consequently, are more likely to spread our brand/product making it known to new users.

Once you get to the advanced level, it is important to start outsourcing your advertising campaigns so that you can focus on other parts of the business. In particular, it is fundamental to outsource the client profiling process. Here are some interesting instructions that can help you speed up the process.

To define the profile of your ideal customer, you have to remember that each individual is influenced by his position in society. Therefore, to trace the profile of the ideal customer, we must answer questions related to these influences.

Social Influences
Cultural Systems and Subsystems

- How old is he?

- Where does he live?

- Is he a man, a woman, or both of them?

- What degree of education does he/she have? What schools did he/she attend?

- What hobbies or passions do they have?

- What are its values?

- What are their beliefs?

Social Class

- What kind of work do they do?

- How much does he or she earn?

Family

- Is he or she married?

- Does he or she have children? How many?

- Does he lives alone and is single?

- Does he live by his parents?

Marketing Influences

- Do they already use a product to meet the need or solve the problem?

- What kind of product do they use?

- What kind of brand?

- What features are relevant?

- What is the benefit most appreciated?

- On what price range is it oriented?

- Is the high price for the customer a way of affirming their social status?

- Do they associate high price with quality?

- What kind of advertising influences their purchase?

- Where do they usually buy?

Situational Influences

- Which environments can influence the purchase (showroom, the point of sale)?

Social Environment

- Within the group in which he/she lives and works, who else influences the choice of purchase?

- Who uses the product?

- Who pays for the product?

- Are the influencer, the consumer, and the buyer the same person?

Psychological Aspects Associated with the Product

- What are their fears?

- What problems do they want to solve?

- What consequences would it entail for an unsolved problem?

- What are the challenges they're facing?

- What are their wishes?

Emotional Aspects Related to the Choice of the Product

- What mistakes are they afraid to commit by making a wrong choice?

- What would it mean for the customer to choose a wrong product?

Now that you have answered these questions, you can trace the profile of the ideal customer.

Here's how to proceed: put a face to your potential client (download a photo from the internet that identifies the physical characteristics of your potential customer) and a fictitious name. Then, compile the data that will trace the characteristics of socio-demographic, psycho-graphic, and consumer experiences. This serves to have a clear representation of him/her with whom we are going to talk and with whom we want to relate.

This exercise can lead to a great transformation to your company; in fact, it will help you understand the motivating beliefs, fears, and secret desires that influence the purchase decisions of the customer. It also tunes your marketing efforts and helps you understands what solutions to offer to your market.

A great resource to boost this process and find people that met your avatar standards on Facebook is lookup-id.com. Thanks to this website, you can define your target customer through the definition of personal characteristics and get a list of people that met them.

Here is how it works.

Once you have entered the website, go on the "Extract Members" section. It is very easy to find on the top right of the page. From there, you want to insert the ID of a Facebook in your niche, which of course will contain people in target with your offer. The website will give you a complete and detailed list of the people in the group, which means that you have just discovered a goldmine, since those will be in target for what you are offering.

On this website, you can even use the FB Search function. Once you have designed the features of your typical prospect, you can insert them in this platform to get a list of users that meet those standards. It is pretty straight forward and it is very easy to use. Our suggestion is to play around with the website and get a grasp of its potential: once you start using it, you will never get back at the classic manual research.

Now, it is time to use another great tool to make life easier and start gathering a following. First of all, install Toolkit for Facebook by PlugEx.

What is this? It is an amazing tool that will allow you to do multiple actions in a matter of seconds. For instance, once you have your list and have launched Toolkit by PlugEx, you can then invite all those people to put a like on your page or to join your group.

When you start using these tools on a regular basis, you will be amazed at how easy it is to grow your fan base and start getting significant results. One little tip that we like to give our readers is to always use a secondary account for this operations in order to guarantee proper privacy protection.

Facebook Advertising 2019

Chapter 8:

A Practical Example

A Practical Example

Now that we have seen how to use the two software in theory, it is time to dive into the practice and use a practical example to understand the concepts better.

So, let's say that we have a shop that sells running gear and we want to find customers that are in target with the items we sell. The first thing we want to do is to go on running groups, like this one https://www.facebook.com/groups/TrailAndUltraRunning/ and look for the group ID. We can do that by going to https://lookup-id.com/ and entering the previous URL. This will give us the ID of the group. After that, we just need to paste the group ID in https://lookup-id.com/get_facebookid.php to get a list of all the members that are inside the group.

After having done that, you can use Toolkit for Facebook by PlugEx to quickly invite all the people on the list you just found to leave a like on your dedicated running store page. Furthermore, you can even invite them in your very own group, where you will start your marketing process.

This is how you can use the two software together to really boost up your experience.

Another great thing you can outsource is the retargeting phase. Once you have acquired a potential client, you can use an automated bot to close the sale for you. Here are some suggestions we found very valuable.

If you're not using ManyChat, right now, you're losing 60% of new potential customers—you're literally burning your money!

Does this seem absurd?

Perhaps you do not know that the chatbots are the future of marketing. Soon, we will see together what they are. For now, know that they have incredible power: to enter people's lives like never before.

Of course, there are e-mails, but, think about it: would anyone really open a promotional e-mail?

The truth is that, for some people, they almost automatically discard e-mails when they find them in the mailbox. They have developed a natural tendency to delete promotional emails.

Associate the email with invasive advertising at work or, again, at the studio. To talk to a friend, however, they use WhatsApp or Facebook Messenger.

WHAT DO WE WANT TO SAY?

You should choose the tool to use based on your audience. If, for example, it is made up of managers, who often check e-mail, e-mail marketing may be the ideal choice.

But, if perhaps, you turn to students, on average 20 years, who have much more convenience with the chat, it would be better to think of a Facebook Bot.

Do you understand what the extraordinary advantage is?

It will allow you to establish an authentic communication with your (potential or not) customer, who will open your message just like a friend. You will receive a notification on your mobile phone who can chat with you—everything automatically.

The only thing you will have to deal with is the bot settings.

The good news is that it is an extremely simple operation. Thanks to the services available, you will use more or less 10 minutes.

However, without knowing how to use this very powerful tool effectively, you would risk undermining this work. This is why in this chapter, we will introduce you to the correct configuration of a chatbot with ManyChat.

Are you ready? Let's start!

WHAT IS MANYCHAT AND HOW TO CREATE A FACEBOOK BOT IN 10 MINUTES

We can say that a bot is a program that can manage automatic and natural conversations in a chat with users. It can answer questions, offer solutions to problems, and make proposals, just as if it were human.

Already from this general definition, you will have guessed that you have in your hands something potentially revolutionary for you and your business. You will free your time, increasing your results.

This year, chatbots and Facebook advertising will go hand-in-hand, so it is very important to learn how to use them properly. Here is a quick guide on how to create a Facebook bot in just 10 minutes!

MANYCHAT, WHAT IS IT?

In short, it is the simplest and most intuitive service to create a Facebook Messenger Bot.

You do not need programming knowledge. The configuration is extremely fast and you will immediately have the opportunity to carry out a series of actions:

- Create automated message sequences

- Send a message to all users registered in the bot

- Use advanced tools to increase conversions

HOW MANYCHAT WORKS: THE 2 BASIC TOOLS FOR BOT MARKETING

We have just said that ManyChat is the easiest to use Messenger Marketing tool. Despite its simplicity, however, it offers a number of features that make it complete and effective for your web marketing strategy.

Do you want some examples?

- *Automatic Sequences*

This is the series of messages that, automatically, ManyChat will send to the user. You can set them as you like, based on your lead generation strategy.

- *Growth Tools*

Here, this is the real bomb among the tools offered. They are a series of "extensions" that add functionality to ManyChat. The most famous is Facebook Comments Tool, which allows you to convert whoever comments on a particular post into a member of the bot.

These are just some of the features you'll have available.

Well, to make you better understand the functioning of a chatbot, let's assume a case of real use:

The user Luke comments on the post of your product with the specific keyword that you have set. Your bot turns on and automatically sends your opt-in message, basically, a welcome message to confirm the user's interest.

Subsequently, based on the behavior of Luke, the bot will send him different messages to achieve the goals you have set. These messages are part of an "automated sequence" that you created earlier.

The important thing is to never be intrusive—keep this in mind during the setup phase. Each time you send a message, a notification will be sent to Luke's mobile phone. This means two things:

- You will enter in his daily life; and

- You will have to manage this opportunity in the best way, so as not to frustrate him (most people are not accustomed to this tool just yet, so do not overuse it).

CONCLUSION

Thank you for making it to the end of *Facebook Advertising*. We hope it was able to provide you with all the tools you need to achieve your goals whatever they may be.

The next step is to get started with what you have learned during the course of this book. Remember to always start by building an audience and creating a positive vibe on your pages: it will make all the difference down the line.

We hope that you find these lessons valuable and that you got the information you were looking for. Creating a "social media lifestyle" that works for you will give you an incredible feeling, especially at the beginning, when you make the first gains. We are thrilled for you to start and we cannot wait to see your results coming in.

To your success!

Finally, if you found this book useful in any way, a review on Amazon is always appreciated!

CPSIA information can be obtained
at www.ICGtesting.com
Printed in the USA
LVHW111349040319
609412LV00001B/137/P